D1083785

SKIPPER SUPREME

SKIPPER SUPREME

Buck Showalter and the Baltimore Orioles

TODD KARPOVICH AND JEFF SEIDEL

FOREWORD BY JASON LA CANFORA

SPORTS
PUBLISHING

Sports Publishing books may be purchased in bulk at special discounts for sales promotion, corporate gifts, fund-raising, or educational purposes. Special editions can also be created to specifications. For details, contact the Special Sales Department, Sports Publishing, 307 West 36th Street, 11th Floor, New York, NY 10018 or sportspubbooks@skyhorsepublishing.com.

Sports Publishing® is a registered trademark of Skyhorse Publishing, Inc.®, a Delaware corporation.

Visit our website at www.sportspubbooks.com.

10 9 8 7 6 5 4 3 2 1

Library of Congress Cataloging-in-Publication Data is available on file.

Interior photos © Mitchell Layton

Cover design by Tom Lau
Cover photo credit AP Images

ISBN: 978-1-61321-839-6
Ebook ISBN: 978-1-61321-840-2

Printed in the United States of America

Contents

A Note from the Authors

Everything turned around inside the House of the Orioles when Buck Showalter took over as manager late in the 2010 season. He not only energized the franchise, but he galvanized the city. He succeeded because of his baseball acumen, and because of his leadership skills. This book delves into both of those qualities. The Orioles weren't taken very seriously for more than a decade before Showalter arrived. They certainly are now.

We've covered most of the home games the last three seasons and many in the years before that, getting to see and hear a number of things that helped us put together a story of how Showalter first changed the culture and then changed their play on the field. This team now relies heavily on pitching, defense, and power. Dan Duquette has been able to give Showalter enough tools to make the changes.

The bottom line is that Showalter has been a driving force since coming to town.

Showalter's still looking for that World Series ring, though. It looked like he might get it in 2014 before the Orioles ran into a buzz saw from Kansas City. The Orioles were so close there and even had home field advantage in the ALCS. But it didn't work out, and then not much went right in 2015.

Still, we had fun writing this book. The research, discussions, and endless e-mails helped give us a pretty good framework for simply explaining what was going on during the last few years. Everyone in the Baltimore media was also always very helpful when we had questions on whatever we were doing. Just a thanks here to everyone, that way we don't leave out names.

From Todd: I would like to thank God, my wife Jill, daughters Wyeth and Marta, my entire family, co-author Jeff Seidel, and colleague Dave Ginsburg for their support through this process.

From Jeff: I want to thank my wife Nadine and kids, my daughter Kara and son Zach. Plus, it was a blast to work with co-author Todd Karpovich and the guidance we got from Mr. Ginsburg was invaluable. The toughest part was keeping our two cats, Buddy and Albie, out of the chair in my office during my numerous late-night typing sessions. But I did it!

Foreword

Buck Showalter gets Baltimore.

He understands its blue collar roots and complicated racial politics and collections of fairly disparate neighborhoods that make up a unique panorama of life. Showalter seems to revel in its provincial tendencies and superstitious nature and rampant inferiority complexes. Innately, he seemed to grasp some of this nuance almost upon arrival and embrace it (his dugout attire seems to be driven by superstition more so than any sense of fashion) and grow to even embody some of these aspects (forever proclaiming "I like our guys," when anyone might point out the chasms between his rosters and some of the AL East behemoths, to say nothing of the gaps in payroll).

Dare I say, in a little over five years in town the man has already secured lifelong "Baltimoron" status. And this, I can attest (as a fervent product of and champion of my city), is indeed a term of significant endearment. Sure, much of it is due to his steady hand in turning a hapless, lifeless franchise back to a vibrant, thriving fulcrum of Maryland summers— restoring it at least somewhere close to its lofty perch as *the* model Major League Baseball franchise from that first World

Series of Brooks and Frank and Palmer in '66 through the Ripken, Murray, and, well, Palmer, incarnation in that last tasted glory in '83. Certainly, those results have a lot to do with it.

But it's also in the way he restored order and class and substance to an organization that seemed devoid of it for so long. It's in the way he sprinkles little tidbits, unprovoked, about rising low-level minor leaguers into questions about that night's opposing starting pitcher, letting you know he's in this for the long haul. It's in the way he protects his players and deals directly with fans and understands some of the limitations of this market and basks in the sanctuary that is Camden Yards. And for as much as I've respected and admired the man for all of that for quite some time now, never was he more an ambassador for Baltimore than this past summer.

With some areas of the city literally burning and the casualty vampires that are the 24-hour news networks entrenched all around the Inner Harbor—a Chris Davis moon shot or two from Buck's very office—looking to exploit the riots for all the fodder they could, Showalter acted with reasoned dexterity. One a spring night when some were wondering exactly when and how the players and fans might get home from that night's game (our son Rocco was to be there as part of a birthday party that was scuttled as roads were closed and traffic rerouted), Showalter was at the ready.

His team would be asked to do what, in baseball terms, constituted significant concessions—play a home game before an empty stadium and then travel to Tampa to play what would be considered a "home" series with the Rays—but what, in the prism of a city torn apart by racial strife and gross inequality and with decades of mistrust of the Baltimore City Police Department now spilling unbridled into the streets, amounted to far less. The depth and complexity of the situation was never lost on the manager, who was the voice of the franchise throughout the ordeal. He was a calming presence of sorts at a time when chaos abounded in the aftermath of the death of Freddie Gray.

In an era when pro sports is the biggest of businesses and can often be cold and distant and far too calculated or inhuman, Buck was a resident of this bleeding city first, a sympathetic voice of reason second, and a baseball manager, perhaps, third. His remorse and his compassion, at least in some small way, helped to diffuse some of the outward hostility, and his words and actions in this time of crisis helped further restore the compact between this team and this town (for years fans railed against the Orioles not wearing "Baltimore" in script on road jerseys and at various times in the past thirty years fears about some outsider—and worst of all, Washingtonian—buying and moving the team have been quite robust).

I grew to further appreciate Showalter's covenant with Baltimore later that season, getting a chance to chat with him for a while during batting practice of an O's game in Detroit. It was clear that for all that Showalter seemed to get about Baltimore, the scope of his job limited his ability to explore the area as much as he would like. Sure, he knew of a few legendary restaurants but swore he pretty much knew only a few ways to get back home from the stadium and was more than happy to have most meals come from his wife, Angela's, handiwork or the ballpark itself. His charitable reach in Baltimore is wide—KidsPeace is one of many outreach projects close to his heart; his annual Halloween Trick-or-Trot 5K and 1 Mile Walk has become a big hit as well—but I got the sense that a lot of what he's astutely gleaned about this city he picked up through osmosis, from being a good listener, from being a diligent and alert reader of people and situations, a byproduct of being a baseball lifer as a coach and player (and therefore an ever-moving professional vagabond).

He could see how generations of families might never move more than a few city blocks apart, and how the very nature of the rowhomes, basically sharing a wall, literally inter-connect the landscape. The glean in his eye as I talked of my grandfather, finishing the workday at Bethlehem Steel, pick-ing up a six-pack (or two) of Natty Boh's and a dozen of crabs in a paper bag from the original Obrycki's on the corner of Pratt and Register, with Chuck Thompson calling the Ori-oles game on the radio in the background somewhere, spoke volumes. This is a city where when you ask someone where they went to school, you mean high school, not college. This is Smalltimore, where everyone from the owner of the baseball team to Michael Phelps to Josh Charles seems to be connected by some acquaintance or family member or bartender; where everyone knows everyone else; and where Buck Showalter just seems to fit right in with us all.

So while this 2015 may not have been filled with some of the outward baseball thrills from the previous few years—the first division title in forever, winning a playoff series, the Delmon Young double, and the J. J. Hardy slide into home plate—it just may have been the perfect setting to capture this man, and this team, in full. The season will remain very memorable in so many other ways, as much for what it said about team's place in the city as the games actually played. It was a somewhat tortured summer, but one that revealed the true character of Showalter and veterans like Adam Jones, who seem to relish their role in the Baltimore community as much as their manager does.

And in the hands of these two gifted and meticulous authors, it's a story very well told, indeed. Todd Karpovich (my first cousin who has always been more of a big brother and, who, yes, grew up literally two blocks away from me in row-homes our parents still call home) is a proud son of Baltimore as well. His passion for writing, relentless appetite for reading, and passion for covering sports in this town could not be any more voracious. He considers it a privilege to call the press-box his office, he is painstaking in the care he takes with his reporting, and this is a story he was born to tell. I've been lucky enough to know Jeff Seidel since our time together at *The Washington Post* far longer ago than either of us would like to admit at this point, and Jeff brings decades of chops covering sports around the state with him offering a perspective a little more outside the incestuous bounds of the city as well.

They were there—in the clubhouse, on the field, in the manager's office—every day during what has been surely one of Buck's more trying seasons. It was one in which the limitations of the roster and its inflexibility must have been handcuffing. It was a year in which seemingly every move the front office made seemed to fail (usually miserably), with the endless strings of "designated for assignment" designations starting mere weeks into the season culminating in a botched attempt to both buy and sell at the trade deadline. This was a team without real regular corner outfielders, with a catcher who could only catch occasionally because he was coming off an injury, without a traditional leadoff hitter, and chronically bereft of on-base percentage prowess. In fact, this team seemed to go two months without a hit with runners in scoring position and with a starting rotation in tatters. Nevertheless, these Orioles remained largely viable until the final weeks of the season.

Coming off the first trip to the ALCS since 1997, with expectations higher than they had been since equally as long, the 2015 Baltimore Orioles were not a success. But they'll be remembered, over time, I suggest, rather fondly, for their collective resilience in a challenging climate. And as much as the losses and the games that got away will consume Buck Showalter deep through this winter, I hope he can find some solace in the way he and his team resonated with this city, in how it responded to a civic crisis, and how it brought ample spirit, and a little joy, at a time when Baltimore so greatly needed it.

—Jason La Canfora, CBS Sports, Winter 2015–16

Chapter One
WHY DID BUCK STOP HERE?

The Baltimore Orioles did not scare a whole lot of teams in the first months of the 2010 season. After all, why should they have? This was a team that featured a roster loaded with has-beens, players who never would be, as well as others who simply hadn't gotten there yet. This group of Orioles had a losing record from the first day of the season, dropped 11 of their first 12 games, and eventually fell to 41 games under the .500 mark on August 1.

People probably hadn't expected much more from this bunch or this franchise. The Orioles had last made the playoffs in 1997, also the last time they could muster a winning record. They went through a revolving door of managers, including Ray Miller, Mike Hargrove, Lee Mazzilli, Sam Perlozzo, Dave Trembley, and Juan Samuel (on an interim basis) from 1998 to 2010. However, no one could seem to figure out how to match the right manager with the right talent.

The Orioles once had been a very proud franchise, one that many in baseball looked up to, tried to resemble, or even both. When Baltimore dominated the American League from the mid-60s through 1983 when it won a third World Series championship, the song remained the same. The Orioles built teams that relied heavily on power, pitching, and defense. Long-time manager Earl Weaver often professed his love for the three-run homer; finding a chance to work with players like Frank Robinson, Boog Powell, Ken Singleton, Lee May, Eddie Murray and others, the Hall of Fame skipper saw plenty of those round-trippers.

The Orioles also showcased some of the best starting rotations and defenses seen in baseball. If the Orioles weren't the best in those areas, then they were awfully close. How do you sneak a ground ball through the left side of the infield that's guarded by Brooks Robinson at third and Mark Belanger at short? There also were guys like Paul Blair roaming around in center while the number of Gold Gloves simply kept piling up. Pitchers like Jim Palmer also were marvelous at fielding their positions.

Another reason for the team's success during those years is that they built and kept a farm system stocked with amazing talent. The Orioles often developed players who took longer to get a chance at the major league level simply because the players there were just too good. Don Baylor and Bobby Grich both went on to become huge impact players in the majors, but both needed to wait until the Orioles could find a spot for them before they could flourish. Baylor eventually was traded away and won an American League Most Valuable Player with the Angels in 1979—the same team Grich had signed with as a free agent in 1976 after he captured MVP honors three times during his tenure with the Orioles.

Grich won four Gold Gloves at second base with the Orioles and made two All-Star appearances before leaving to go back home to California. But those were the types of players the Orioles routinely drafted and developed during those years. To this ball club, it was a very simple game. When the major league players could not do the job anymore, there'd usually be someone at Triple-A Rochester who could answer the bell.

That system seemed to break down when the free-agent era began in the late 1970s. The Yankees got the ball rolling by signing players like Catfish Hunter and Reggie Jackson during that time. They kept signing players even though they were already arguably baseball's strongest team during that time period. Relief pitcher Sparky Lyle, a left-hander, won the American League Cy Young Award with the Yankees in 1977, but the team decided to go out and sign dominant right-handed relief pitcher Rich Gossage in the off-season. Why? The basic feeling then seemed to be well, just because they could. And so they did.

The Orioles eventually jumped into that market a few years later, but also their farm system seemed to stop producing talented players at the rate that it had during the glory years. Baltimore began to show signs of a downward spiral in the mid-1980s. Though the Orioles still won at times, it was an up and down situation over the next several years before losing became the norm beginning with the 1998 season when Miller took over as the manager. Many thought the Orioles would be fine that year, as they had won the American League East title the previous year and made the playoffs the season before that under Davey Johnson. But everything fell apart when Johnson walked away. Starting in 1998, and the Orioles posted a losing record for the next fourteen seasons, showing few signs of improvement along the way.

The 2010 season might have been one of the worst. Manager Dave Trembley began the season on the hot seat, one that grew even warmer right from the start of spring training. The Orioles dropped nine in a row in the first few weeks and slid to 1–11 during that stretch. They finally made their move and fired Trembley after going 15–39 to open the season. Samuel took over as the interim skipper, and the team went 17–34 even though the players seemed to like him and play hard. There just wasn't much progress being made.

Baltimore appeared to be heading on a swift ride to nowhere when Buck Showalter accepted the team's offer to become the manager with about two months left in the season. The Orioles were 32–73, the worst record in the majors, with no hope in sight. Up to that point, the team had never played well for any kind of long stretch that season.

Showalter had taken over losing teams before or managed young teams that couldn't quite get it done. He became manager of the 1992 Yankees, a team really loaded with good young players, at the age of thirty-six and guided them to the playoffs three years later. Owner George Steinbrenner, according to various reports, fired Showalter after that 1995 season because the manager would not let go of some coaches. Joe Torre took over the team the next season, and the Yankees won four World Series titles in the next five seasons.

After the Yankees, Showalter moved over to Arizona and helped start that team during its inaugural season in 1998. The D-backs won 100 games in their second year and made it to the National League playoffs but lost to the Mets in the National League Division series, three games to one. Showalter was fired the next season despite the team's 85–77 record. And what happened the year after that? Bob Brenly took over the team and won the World Series over the Yankees in a memorable seven-game battle.

Showalter then moved to the Rangers and took over that team in 2003. He stayed there for four years before being let go after the 2006 season. He earned Manager of the Year honors for the second time, in 2004, when the Rangers improved from 71 wins the previous season to 85, but still found himself without a team after four years in Texas.

He then wound up at ESPN as one of the network's many analysts. Showalter became popular there due to his

Orioles manager Buck Showalter—who used to manage Texas—talks with then-Rangers manager Ron Washington before a 2014 game.

self-deprecating humor and ability to analyze just about any situation. He remained out of baseball for the next three seasons before things began to change during 2010 while Samuel remained in charge of the Orioles. The team looked for a more experienced manager to take command. Showalter's name landed in that mix, and eventually the job went to him at the end of July.

"Buck Showalter's proven track record makes him the right choice for manager of the Orioles," then-president of baseball operations Andy MacPhail said in a statement. "We believe Buck's extensive experience and expertise will be a major benefit to us as we look towards a more successful future."

Showalter made a similar statement before taking the reins, saying that "my job with ESPN allowed me to follow this organization closely over the last several years, and although the current record may seem to indicate otherwise, I see enormous potential with this club. I look forward to the challenge of competing in the American League East.

Baltimore is a tremendous baseball town with passion and pride in its club, and my family and I look forward to making it our new home."

A story on the Bleacher Report website in October, 2014 talked about the fact that there actually had been some discussion on letting Showalter simply take over the team the following year, rather than in 2010, a season that already was long gone. MacPhail said that he wanted Showalter to step in right there in early August in order to get a real good look of who and what the Orioles were. The thinking was that that way, he could do even more in 2011. That turned out to be the right move as Showalter immediately threw himself into everything.

Just like a good card player, who always knows his hand, Showalter wanted to fully understand all the pieces to the puzzle that made up the Orioles so he could be prepared to help the team improve. MacPhail had worked hard to rebuild the once-dominant Baltimore farm system and made several moves that really laid the foundation for greater things. He emphasized the importance of being prepared for games, which is why, according to the players, things began to change pretty quickly.

"The impact was immediate," MacPhail said in that Bleacher Report story. "One thing I was impressed with was the level of preparation. It's really outstanding. The level of preparation to help players' performance is the best I've been around at that level. He works extremely hard. I think the players understand he wants them to be the best they can be. They took to it right away."

The Orioles started the Showalter era on August 3 of that season with a three-game home series against the Angels, who came into the series struggling a bit but still with a 54–53 record under long-time manager Mike Scioscia. Things began changing in Baltimore right away as the Orioles swept the series and started a streak where they won eight of the first nine games under their new manager. Angels outfielder Torii Hunter said he noticed a change in the Orioles during that first series.

"These guys got a second wind with Buck Showalter coming in, they had a little life. I've been watching these guys on TV, they're totally different these last three games," Hunter said that week. "They've been hitting some good pitching, swinging the bats well, hitting doubles, hitting homers. A lot of guys they're doing their thing, stepping up. Of course we're playing bad baseball, but at the same time, coming in we felt pretty confident, we took two out of three at Texas, and they shut that down. I think it's a little bit of spark they have over there right now. You've got to give them credit when credit's due."

Showalter helped right the listing ship, and the Orioles simply took off the rest of the way that season. Baltimore went 34–23 after he took over the job, following their 32–73 start. That's a big change, and it's one that caught many people's attention. The new skipper paid extra attention to detail in so many ways and in and people in baseball often think they've seen it all.

One good example of this is what happened on August 21, 2010. Showalter's Orioles played the Rangers in a late-afternoon game that started at 4:10 p.m. at Camden Yards. Texas sat in first place in the American League West at the time, while the Orioles were just starting to get on to their feet. Baltimore banged out 11 hits and handed the Rangers an 8–6 loss in a game that lasted two hours and 45 minutes, ending just before 7:00 p.m. Meanwhile, the franchise's Double-A team in Bowie was starting a game against the Richmond Flying Squirrels (yes, that's their name) about 30 minutes from Camden Yards, and team officials had been alerted to expect a visitor from Baltimore.

"We were told in the afternoon that there was a possibility Buck might show up if the stars align well in Baltimore, and he could make it down in time," said Bowie assistant general manager Phil Wrye.

The reason Showalter wanted to come to Bowie? Relief pitcher Jim Johnson, who later became the Orioles' closer, would be pitching in a rehab assignment with the Baysox that night. At that time, elbow tendinitis had sidelined Johnson for nearly three months, and the big right-hander was set to throw for a second straight game. Showalter wanted to see Johnson pitch and decided to take a short trip and watch.

Everything worked out fine because the Baysox penciled in Johnson to throw the sixth inning, and that gave Showalter some extra time to reach the stadium. But he arrived before the top of the fifth inning, and Wrye remembered Showalter entering quietly through the team's clubhouse down the right-field line and then walking along that line to their first-base dugout. He then stood there in the corner of the dugout—in uniform, wearing a team jacket—and watched.

"I was very impressed by it," Wrye said. "This guy just took over a major league team . . . [and] he's got a lot of responsibilities. I thought it was unique that he came in uniform and didn't just sit in the stands. But to come down in that situation after he'd been at Camden Yards managing a game all day. I had never heard of it, and I'd never seen it before or since."

Everyone noticed that the Orioles manager had come to watch their farm team's game after managing his own. As Wrye said, this was an almost unheard-of situation. But to Showalter, there was a purpose to this trip. He wanted to get a look at Johnson and even speak with the pitcher, who eventually became the team's All-Star closer a few years later.

"He throws good," Showalter said the next day. "He's getting close. That's one of the reasons why I wanted to see it. It was good."

Said Wrye: "He just wanted to see his guy throw up close and personal."

The visit to watch Johnson exemplifies one way in which Showalter did his research. He wanted to know who the players were and how everything worked.

Showalter also talked with Earl Weaver, the legendary manager who guided the Orioles to the World Series four times and earned a spot in the Hall of Fame. The new skipper loved talking to the legendary skipper, in what appeared to be strong efforts on Showalter's part to try to build a kind of new appreciation for and pride in the franchise.

In fact, when the Orioles unveiled a statue of Weaver, several of Showalter's players came and quietly sat in front and watched, trying hard not to draw attention to themselves but showing respect for a man who made this franchise into something. Showalter understood that history, and it's probably why he enjoyed just talking to Weaver.

"I think the biggest thing is he had time for me," Showalter said before the 2013 home opener. "He didn't have to. You could tell how much the Orioles meant to him."

As time went on, Showalter seemed to achieve a similar status to Weaver in Baltimore—as the man who could do no wrong. In fact, the Orioles scheduled a giveaway for Buck Showalter gnomes midway through the 2015 season, and the results genuinely stunned the manager. There were lines around the block for that night's game and, before the game even ended, people were offering to sell them on the Internet for good money. After the game, when told this, all the skipper could do was shake his head in amazement.

As Showalter's status changed, so too did the Orioles' status on the field seem to change. The team quickly grew into a competitive, fighting group. The Orioles had been pushed around, out-managed, outplayed, and out-everythinged for so long. That just was not happening anymore.

Despite their 69–93 record in 2011, the Orioles showed clear improvement on the field. They were right around .500

for the first half of the season before fading in July and August. Still, they played better in September and helped knock the Red Sox out of the playoffs by rallying for a walk-off 4–3 victory, the season's final win. That seemed to set the stage for 2012, the year everything turned around.

The Orioles pushed hard in September and earned a wild-card spot in the 2012 playoffs. They upset Texas in that one-game series on the road and pushed the Yankees to the limit in a divisional series, as New York needed five games to win the best-of-five affair. They did not make a playoff appearance in 2013, but the Orioles took another step up in 2014. They took off in the second half of the season and ran away from the American League East, easily winning that division by 12 games thanks to a 96–66 record. Baltimore swept Detroit in the best-of-five divisional series before the upstart Royals stunned the Orioles with a four-game sweep in the American League Championship Series.

All of that success made Showalter wildly popular in Baltimore. It also brought the Orioles a very long way from where they were when Showalter took over in 2010. Dan Duquette took over for MacPhail in 2012, and he worked with Showalter to masterfully manipulate the roster throughout the season to give the Orioles the needed pieces at the right time. Both won national honors in 2014, and the city fell in love with the Orioles again. That set the high expectations for the 2015 season; even though not many moves were made in the off-season, many expected the Orioles to win. Still, they finished with a discouraging 81–81 record. In just a few short years, Showalter made mediocrity a disappointment.

Chapter Two

THE DETAILS

The managing style of Buck Showalter with the Orioles has been built heavily upon what he's seen and learned throughout his career: obtain and analyze details to the utmost degree and make decisions based upon that. When Earl Weaver ran the Orioles, he was one of the first—if not *the* first—manager to keep the stats that every team does today. He simply kept statistics about how every player hit against every pitcher. Those numbers often showed odd things, like the fact that certain players who weren't the greatest hitters would nail guys who were really good pitchers. Why? Who knows? But the numbers did not lie.

Though baseball truly has changed a lot in the past ten to twenty years, Showalter, like Weaver, seems to believe heavily in details to help him make the decisions that he feels are best for his team—decisions that might not always be "by the book." That, however, is the hard part of being a manager and one of the things that Showalter seems to do best.

One of the moves that Showalter will long be remembered for came when he was managing the Arizona Diamondbacks on May 28, 1998. The D-backs, struggling with a 16–36 record, were holding on to an 8–6 lead in the ninth inning of a game against the San Francisco Giants with Barry Bonds coming to the plate and the bases loaded. So Showalter made a move that shocked everyone.

He told pitcher Gregg Olson to intentionally walk Bonds, with the bases loaded. Now, what makes this even more interesting is that at that point Bonds had yet to start posting those monumental home run numbers that baseball fans would love. Perhaps even more interesting is that Bonds had not been knocking the ball all over the ballpark that night. In fact, he did not even start. He came on as a pinch-hitter in the eighth inning and drew a regular walk. Nevertheless, he was a very dangerous power hitter. So when the Giants threatened again in the ninth, Bonds got that bases-loaded walk, which the two teams said then was the first time a move like that had been made in the majors since 1944.

The unusual move worked, as Olson then got the next hitter, Brent Mayne, on a line drive to right field, ending the game and preserving an 8–7 victory. Bonds clearly was not happy with the move. In an article in the *San Francisco Chronicle* two days later, Bonds said he still wasn't sure what to say about it.

"I've had a whole night to think about it, and I still don't know what to say," Bonds said. "I don't know how to put it into words. Buck made history. Let him discuss it."

But Showalter's reaction that day was typical for him, a philosophical shrug of the shoulders.

"Wouldn't it be nice and refreshing if people thought about it in the same way whether it worked or not?" he said in the article. "Just because it hasn't been done is no reason to do it or don't do it. That gave us the best opportunity to win the game."

That's the key. He felt the move—unusual as it was—gave the D-backs the best chance to win that game that day. That's what Showalter always is looking for. What lets my team have the best chance for success? Sometimes it leads to unconventional moves, or decisions that look unusual. If Showalter thinks the decision could work, he'll consider it.

He made a similar move in the 2014 American League Division Series against Detroit, which is detailed later in this book, but the gist is that Showalter instructed his pitcher to put the winning run on base in the bottom of the ninth inning, rather than pitching to Nick Castellanos, a solid hitter. Of course, that move could have turned the series around if Detroit, down two games to none, had won. But he believed in the move and it worked out when the next batter, Hernan Perez, hit into a double play. Again, it was about what would give the Orioles the best opportunity to win the game, rather than proceeding with the more popular move.

A few weeks before, though, Showalter made a move that had a few people scratching their heads. When the Orioles took on the Yankees in Derek Jeter's last home game in late September, they had nothing to lose. Baltimore already had the division wrapped up with a playoff spot waiting. But the Orioles and Showalter ran into an interesting situation when Jeter came to bat with one out in the bottom of the ninth inning of a tie game. The Yankees had a runner on second base, and the smart baseball move seemed to be walking Jeter to set up a double play or at least a force play to get out of the inning.

Except that the Orioles elected to pitch to Jeter, who got the game-winning single moments later. There had been some who wondered if Showalter, who was Jeter's first major league manager, didn't walk the shortstop knowing it could have been his last at-bat at Yankee Stadium, which it wound up being. During the 2015 season, an MLB Network documentary about Showalter brought up the question. Showalter half-smiled and looked at host Bob Costas with a very simple answer.

"I'd never tell . . . it ended well for everybody, how's that?" Showalter replied, asking what else they'd like to discuss.

Showalter's players seem to have extreme confidence in the skipper's abilities to make the right moves at the right times, but even more than that, they appear to believe in his ability to supply them the best information so that they can play to the best of their abilities. Some managers used to call it something like "playing hunches," but now, with so much information available to teams and players and management from so many sources, it offers detail-happy people like Showalter a chance to analyze even more and make moves they are comfortable with.

"He will bring up things [in the advanced meetings] and we're like, 'OK, never thought of it that way,'" said infielder/outfielder Steve Pearce in an MLB.com article during the 2014 postseason. "He gives his team the best shot to win. It seems like every move he makes, it works out. Even as a player, there's stuff he thinks of that you don't."

Nelson Cruz expressed similar thoughts about the skipper in the same October 2014 MLB.com article, talking about how Showalter's intelligence plays a big role for the team because he keeps making the right calls and pushing the right buttons.

"Nobody gave us a shot to be AL East champs, and here we are, the second-best record in the American League," Cruz said. "I think he is one of the best managers in baseball and a very smart guy."

Showalter was fortunate to learn from some great coaches and managers, one of whom was the late Billy Martin. Bill Pennington's book *Billy Martin: Baseball's Flawed Genius* tells several stories about how Martin, one of the greatest managers of his time in baseball despite all of his troubles, showed Showalter a thing or two about the game. Showalter, then thirty-one, worked with Martin's Yankees during the spring of

Orioles manager Buck Showalter walks around as his team works out before a game. He likes to know everything that's going on all the time.

1988 and saw a few things about the game and learned about what to watch for if he wanted to be a manager.

"He taught me to have my eyes darting everywhere, looking for something to use later in a game," Showalter said in the book.

In the book, Pennington also details how Showalter helped out Martin and the Yankees in a spring game with one small piece of information. New York was playing the Chicago White Sox in a game that moved into the 10th inning. The Yankees had Bobby Meacham on first base when Chicago brought in a pitcher named Ken Patterson, who used to be in the New York system.

Martin then began yelling in the dugout to see if anyone knew this pitcher. Showalter was very familiar with him because he'd managed Patterson the year before, so Martin queried him about what kind of move to first base this pitcher had. Well, it turned that there was a bit of a story behind that, one that Showalter let Martin know about.

"I told Billy that Patterson actually has a phobia about throwing to first base," Showalter said in the book. "He can't do it."

After that, Martin yelled out to his first-base coach to make the pitcher throw over. Meacham took a small lead of about four feet and then six feet, but Patterson just faked a throw to first. Martin screamed to take a bigger lead. Meacham moved the lead to eight feet and eventually twelve.

Eventually, as Showalter explained in the book, Patterson threw it, but it sailed over the first baseman's head, sending Meacham to third base.

The Orioles under Showalter also have adjusted their thinking with regards to defense, a subject that's gone in a different direction in the past few seasons in the major leagues. Teams always worried about batters that would hit the ball certain ways, a person who was a dead-pull hitter, for example. But how to defend them? Teams were very wary of doing anything extremely different; this is a sport that accepts change gradually, if at all.

Teams slowly began using and then even favoring a variety of shifts. Since sabermetrics and numbers have really found their place in baseball in the last ten years, it's been hard for teams and managers to ignore the fact that some players hit the ball to one area more often than others. Tampa Bay, under former manager Joe Maddon, began using the shifts a lot, and eventually so did the Orioles under Showalter.

"People were doing it years ago," Showalter said in a June 15, 2013, *Baltimore Sun* article. "It's not something new. Ask Willie McCovey [power hitter on the San Francisco Giants with teammate Willie Mays]. But a lot of it then was really tough because you were basing it on just what your gut told you."

The *Sun* reported that the Orioles' use of those various shifts increased 467 percent from 2011 to 2012 and said that the most common use of it was when a team would move the shortstop to the right of second base. It first got a lot of looks when Ted Williams was in his heyday with the Red Sox in the 1940s and '50s. The difference now is that teams employ the shift in a variety of ways. They'll put second basemen halfway between the edge of the infield and where a right fielder would play. That way if a left-handed pull hitter rips a hard ground ball then he could be simply thrown out by that second baseman, even though he's halfway to the right fielder.

A *Wall Street Journal* article on March 27, 2014, talks about how "baseball's approach to defense, long unchanged except for the gloves getting bigger, is undergoing the most radical change in strategy since the Reconstruction Era. Defensive shifting . . . is become epidemic. Major League teams 'shifted' 8,134 times last season, compared with just 2,357 in 2011 . . . the most forward-thinking teams create different schemes and setups for virtually every batter, then switch it up, depending on the pitch count."

Showalter's Orioles have been at the forefront of this trend. The Birds routinely shift in games, sometimes on different counts to the same batter. They'll move the third baseman, the shortstop, the second baseman, and it's all for one thing—to try and save runs. The Orioles have come up with numerous assists over the past few seasons where the third baseman, shortstop, and second baseman are throwing to first from unusual positions. The third baseman could throw from where the second baseman usually works. Same with the shortstop. The second baseman could be almost anywhere, especially with a left-handed hitter who pulls the ball up at the plate. Chris Davis, who joined the Orioles in 2011, has probably seen this too many times already in the past few seasons.

In fact, the Orioles led the major leagues in shifts in 2013 (595) ahead of Tampa Bay (556) and Milwaukee (538), according to the *WSJ* article. It's what Showalter thinks will help the Orioles win, and so far, so good.

Chapter Three
MAKING THE PLAYOFFS

The first steps of the Orioles' turnaround probably began when Showalter took the manager's job in 2010 with the intention of reviving a once-proud franchise that had grown dormant. The 34–23 record that the Orioles posted over the final two months of 2010 was a dramatic increase over what the team had done before that—32–73—and showed that this team certainly could play well. But for how long?

That's what many were trying to figure out when the 2011 season began. Could the Orioles continue their strong play from the final part of 2010? In fact, they did at the start, posting a 30–31 record in the first 61 games before falling apart after that. The Orioles slid throughout the summer and came into the season's final month with a record of 54–80.

But the Orioles slowly began to play better baseball in September. They posted a record of 15–13 that month despite matching up against tough opponents, most from the American League East. After losing four in a row early in the month, the Orioles beat Tampa Bay and the Angels twice each in a three-game series. Then came a surprising series in Boston where the Orioles took three of four from a fast-fading Red

Sox team. In the last series of the season, Boston came to Baltimore and saw the Orioles take two of three in Baltimore.

"We were playing good baseball for the whole month, and it was good to end on a good note and finish off a good, strong finish," Showalter said in a press conference at the winter meetings a few months later. "We didn't take any emotion of somebody else's pain. We were trying to finish up strong. I know our fans enjoyed the competition, respected the way our guys competed the last month. And other than that—we finished up strong the year before. We've won a few more games each year, the last two years, and we need the increments to be bigger."

The way that the final game ended really seemed to give the Orioles a jolt over the winter and into the 2012 season. Boston held a 3–2 lead in the bottom of the ninth with two outs before the Orioles rallied for two runs to stun the Red Sox, 4–3. The Orioles celebrated wildly after that contest, almost like it was their playoff game. Robert Andino got the game-winning hit and made it very clear afterwards how much it meant to him.

"End of season like this, to make Boston go home sad, crying, I'll take it all day," Andino told the media. "To walk off, everybody wants to walk off. It's priceless man, you don't have any words for it. Just enjoy it, and there's no tomorrow, so next year."

That strong September helped set the tone for the 2012 season. It didn't have the same feel as the "Why Not?" season of 1989, where the Orioles battled for first place until the final two games of that season after losing 107 games the year before, but nevertheless the team found itself in the pennant race in 2012. And because of that, the city of Baltimore slowly began to notice and interest picked up. When Showalter was the manager with the D-backs in the 1999 playoffs, he faced a similar situation because that team was brand-new. The Orioles hadn't been near postseason play for 15 years, and some comments Showalter made before his playoff time with Arizona also could have been used with Baltimore.

"I used to think that experience [being in the playoffs] might be a little overrated, but after being through the playoffs in New York, there are a lot of things that catch you off guard," Showalter said back then. "You think the way the fans support you in New York and the passion and everything, a lot like they do here in Phoenix, that there weren't another level that they could take it to, but they did. To be exposed to that type of, call it pressure or what have you, to be able to come through that and function and work underneath those pressures is something that you can't feed off of. You realize how lucky you are to do this for a living. It's very easy to say, 'Okay, guys have fun and relax,' but it's something that's very important to your fans and a lot of things. It's quite a microscope to place players and everybody under."

The Orioles did not travel an easy road to the 2012 playoffs. They did, however, get off to a good start, winning their first three games and never having a losing record at any time. The Orioles remained close to both first place and the wild card throughout the first half of the season before slipping midway through and falling 10 games out of the top spot. They appeared to be en route to yet another losing season before things began to change.

The Orioles heated up in the second half of the season. They won 18 games in August and 19 more in September, scoring victories in all kinds of ways. On one mid-September night in Seattle, for example, the Orioles rallied for two runs in the ninth to force extra innings and eventually pulled out a 4–2 victory in 18 innings. During this game, seven Baltimore relief pitchers combined to throw 12 2/3 scoreless frames while striking out 16 batters. The Orioles pulled closer and closer to the top of the American League East, eventually tying the Yankees for first place in the division in early September, needing just 44 games to wipe out that 10-game deficit.

After catching New York on September 4, the Orioles stayed right there with the Yankees until the season's final weekend. That's when the schedule hurt Baltimore while helping New York. The Yankees faced a three-game series with a Boston Red Sox team that had fallen to pieces in the season's final weeks, whereas the Orioles needed to play a tough Tampa Bay team that had been fighting for first place in the East until the final days.

The Orioles won just one of three in Tampa Bay and wound up two games behind the Yankees to earn a wild-card spot. That put the Orioles on the road against Texas, a team that faded badly in the season's final days. Texas held a five-game lead over Oakland with nine games remaining in the season but then staggered to a 2–7 finish, opening the door for the A's to rally and win the American League West. That collapse clearly upset the Rangers, who many people felt had one of the toughest lineups in the game, and they talked like they could still get it together and make a very good postseason run.

The Orioles, on the other hand, faced a bit of a different situation. They had not made the playoffs in fifteen years. Nobody even vaguely forecasted them to be in the hunt for any kind of postseason bid. The last time they posted a winning record came during that last playoff season in 1997. The team appeared simply happy to be in the playoffs. Despite Showalter's role in Baltimore's success, the fact that the team had made such a major turnaround in two years was something that Showalter made clear he did not want sole credit for.

Showalter routinely talks about the success of a team being about the team. It's not a one-person deal but comes from the hard work of everyone involved. That is what he talked about before the 2012 playoffs.

"It's about the players. I didn't do it," Showalter said. "I had good players, general manager, scouts, our front office. It's just unfortunate in our society we want to hang the golden hero around somebody. It doesn't fit in this case. With our team it's just a bunch of guys that raised the bar and wouldn't give in and still haven't. Now they get a chance to win to roll the dice, and there's a lot of good card players in there."

Showalter also talked about how he realized that the "shelf life" of coaches and managers in sports works out. After all, he'd been fired three times after helping turn those teams around. He'd just done the same thing with the Orioles in a little over two years but still was looking down the road, while also trying to enjoy what this team had done.

"You're just thankful for every opportunity you get and hope in some form you've impacted them the way they've impacted me," he said. "We all grow through life's experiences, so without getting too deep, I was real thankful for the opportunity I got here and continue to be."

Showalter said that he was proud of how the 2012 Orioles came together as a team. The Orioles of that season featured a number of players who could cause a number of problems. They did not ride the coattails of just one or two players to the postseason. There were different players who found ways to give the Orioles a boost when they needed it. That's what championship teams do.

In fact, the Orioles did something else many very good teams do—they won tough and tight games, no matter how long they took. The Orioles lost their first two extra-inning games of the season in April and then won the last 16 they played in during the regular season. In other words, they finished 16–2 in extra-inning games, a stunning statistic that helped them to a playoff berth. They won games that lasted 10, 11, 12, 13, 14, 15, 17, and 18 innings and captured them in different ways.

The 9–6 victory that the Orioles posted in Boston on May 6 might have been both the most unique and one that the team looked back on as a bit of a jumping-off point. That game took 17 innings and featured the unusual scenario wherein both teams literally ran out of pitchers. Showalter turned to Chris Davis, who played both the infield and the outfield and had pitched some during his collegiate days.

Davis nearly gave up a run in the 16th on a two-out double from Mike Aviles, but center fielder Adam Jones made a perfect relay throw to shortstop J. J. Hardy, who gunned down Marlon Byrd at the plate to keep the game going. Jones then snapped the 6–6 tie by blasting a three-run homer in the top of the 17th inning off of former Orioles outfielder Darnell McDonald, who was pitching for the Red Sox since Boston also had run out of bullpen arms.

Davis then gave up a single and a walk to start the 17th but struck out power hitter Adrian Gonzalez and got McDonald to ground into a game-ending double play. There were a lot of smiles that day, as it was a victory that so many on the team could take pride in, because so many helped.

"It was bizarre," Jones said in a *Baltimore Sun* article. "It was fun. It was awesome. It was exhausting. It was exhilarating. That was awesome, top to bottom, six hours. Started off right, it ended right, a lot of stuff in between. It's just a big, big win, and it put everybody to an emotional test."

They faced more tests in the playoffs, first having to go on the road for a one-game wild-card matchup with the Rangers. That was the type of team managers don't like to face. Texas had stumbled to the finish line, blown a late-season lead in the American League West, and entered the playoffs as a wild-card team. The talk in the short time before this game for the Rangers seemed to involve focusing on what would happen in the ALDS and maybe ALCS after they beat the Orioles. After all, even though the late-season fade was a bad one, the Rangers still were able to play this game at home.

But the Orioles stunned the Rangers, 5–1, getting a gritty effort from starter Joe Saunders, who took them into the sixth, and scoring the game's final four runs. After the game, Showalter talked about how tough this group had become and the way they'd grown together. Showalter spoke about how much the team wanted to keep advancing because they hoped to play long enough to give injured outfielder Nick Markakis a possible chance to come back.

"There's just a lot of guys that had their noses bloodied together here. They developed a fraternity in there, of people that can play for their team," he said. "The two things that guys have rallied around is trying to get back and play some games at our ballpark in front of our fans and trying to keep winning so Nick Markakis can get a chance to play in the postseason. Each day that passes we get a chance of that."

Markakis was injured when hit by a pitch from Yankees left-hander CC Sabathia in September of that season and suffered a broken thumb. The Orioles hoped the right fielder could somehow make it back for postseason play but it never happened. Still, the Orioles advanced to the American League Division Series, and Showalter talked before Game 1 about how emotional just being in the playoffs is for any team. The Orioles might have been feeling it more than most since fifteen years had elapsed since the last time Baltimore made it.

"You put your heart—the players put their heart on the line every night out there, and they put themselves up to ridicule and—let's face it, we see as many mishaps on highlight reels as we do good things, and that's part of it," Showalter said. "You put yourself out there every night. This is hard to do. What they're being asked to do is hard. That's why they're the best players in the world. That's why this time of year it's a level that a lot of people can only—can't really fathom. That's why

I've always challenged them along the way to stay together because people don't really get the reality of what they're being asked to do or trying to do other than themselves, and they stay together."

And that's probably why the Orioles gave the Yankees such a fight in that series. There were a number of emotional factors at play in the five-game series, from Baltimore's long time without making the playoffs to Showalter having taken the Yankees to the playoffs himself in 1995 before losing his job. The two teams had battled throughout the final part of the regular season for the American League East title, which the Yankees won by two games. That gave New York the home field advantage in the best-of-five series and helped the Yankees clinch it in the final game at Yankee Stadium.

What the Orioles will probably always look back on is how they split the first two games in Baltimore but could have won both. The Orioles played Game 1 just two days after beating Texas in the wild-card game and were tied 2–2 heading into the ninth when closer Jim Johnson came in and just fell apart. Johnson had been a very reliable closer for the Orioles that season, making 51 saves and earning an All-Star selection.

Russell Martin led off the ninth with a tie-breaking home run, and Johnson went on to allow five runs in just one-third of an inning as New York went on to a 7–2 victory. The Orioles, though, wasted a few good scoring chances where they could have taken the lead going into the ninth. They rallied the next night for a 3–2 victory but had to go back to New York for the final three games of the series tied at one, meaning two victories in three games would be needed to advance to the ALCS.

Game 3 is another one that probably kept some of the Orioles and their skipper up at night for a while. The Birds took a 2–1 lead into the bottom of the ninth when Showalter called on Johnson once again, but he stumbled for a second time, giving up a one-out homer to Raul Ibañez that tied the game and forced extra innings. The Yankees eventually won 3–2 in 12 innings.

Showalter would not throw Johnson under the bus after that game. The skipper always is very careful to support and defend his players to the media, something he did following this tough loss.

"Believe me, we'd be at home watching without people like Jim Johnson," Showalter said. "He's a special guy. We're real proud of him, and you'll see him again tomorrow night, I hope."

Showalter was right. The Orioles needed Johnson again the next night, and the right-hander came through in a save situation as Baltimore bounced back to pull out a 2–1 victory in 13 innings. Johnson came on in the 13th inning and retired New York in order. That set up the deciding Game 5, a game where the Orioles could not do much against Sabathia as the Yankees wrapped up the series with a 3–1 victory.

After the game, Showalter spoke at length about how proud he was of this team and what they accomplished, especially because it can be so hard to make the playoffs. Cal Ripken made the World Series in his second full year as an Oriole, but never got back. Showalter took so much pride in the tough, gritty way this group played all season long. Two years before, the Orioles truly had been one of the biggest jokes in baseball. No one was laughing anymore, and their skipper wanted them to be proud of their effort in 2012.

"They have a very well-deserved rest. They are a special group," Showalter said. "You don't know how many times you are going to pass this way, and, you know, they got a grip on— like a lot of young people, they know they are not bulletproof and we talked way back in spring training in our first meeting, and they bought into each other. And they were good team-mates and people that our city and organization can be proud of. And we'll see them again. It's been about as much fun as I have had in the big leagues watching how they play the game every day, the standard they held themselves to and the way they raised the bar in Baltimore with each other."

Chapter Four
THE 2014 SEASON

Many experts predicted that the Orioles would be in the fight for the American League East Division title in 2014 or, at worst, one of the two wild-card spots. They earned a wild-card spot in 2012 and stayed in the hunt for much of 2013 before fading late and not making postseason play.

But everything worked out right for the Orioles in 2014. They started a little slowly, righted the ship midway through, and ran away with the division in the second half. Baltimore ended up with a 96–66 record and won the division by 12 games. After that, the Orioles swept the Tigers in three games in the American League Division Series before the Kansas City Royals surprisingly swept Baltimore in four games in the American League Championship Series. The Orioles wound up one step from the World Series, but they understood how far they came, something Showalter talked about after Kansas City wrapped up the ALCS.

"You know, there's so many roads to cross to get here. And it's not always—it's not always health," Showalter said. "But it's about players and talent and . . . doing the right thing consistently over a long period of time. And holding themselves to a high standard on and off the field."

In fact, the Orioles had been confident from the start that they could make a good run in 2014. The timing was right. They'd been competitive for two straight years, posting a winning record in each of them and showing they could play with anyone. The Orioles also had nearly perfected their unusual way of making moves that kept their bullpen fresh—sending players with options up and down on a regular basis so pitchers either would not get tired or run out of gas. Teams had done this at times, especially in September when the rosters can be expanded, but the Orioles used the format aggressively and did it throughout the season.

Executive Vice President, Baseball Operations Dan Duquette and Showalter had together talked about the numerous moves, but the skipper then stayed busy with them. Showalter got his players to believe in what he was doing and how he did

Orioles manager Buck Showalter talks with Executive Vice President, Baseball Operations Dan Duquette before a game.

it. What really proved interesting was how much the Orioles could feel that their skipper could help them.

"Buck's been amazing from the time he came over to the time we are now," pitcher Bud Norris said during the 2014 playoffs. "I think all the media writers and fan base can understand exactly what happened and where we are. When it comes to baseball and what he gives us players, an opportunity to go out and perform at a high level, he really gets to know each guy on an individual note and gives us the best opportunity to play. That's something you can see when he's moving the rotation around, putting guys in different positions and stuff like that. It gives him a lot of confidence in us, and proves that he has confidence in us, as well. It's been exciting. He lets us go out there and play baseball, and that's what we're here to do."

Showalter has earned a reputation as a very good strategist on the bench. He's not afraid to make moves that could raise a few eyebrows, but more than anything, he wants to put his players in the right spots to succeed, because that success often translates to victories.

One of his boldest moves came in Game 3 of the ALCS against the Tigers. Norris and the Orioles' bullpen had kept the strong Detroit lineup quiet, and Baltimore carried a 2–1 lead into the bottom of the ninth. They were three outs away from winning this series when suddenly, everything started to fall apart.

Closer Zach Britton, who had been consistent throughout the season and already earned a save in Baltimore's stunning come-from-behind 7–6 win in Game 2, came in and got off to a bad start. Victor Martinez and J.D. Martinez started the ninth inning with back-to-back doubles to cut the lead to 2–1 and put a runner in scoring position with no outs. Backup catcher Bryan Holaday, who came on in the sixth inning, tried to get a sacrifice bunt down and couldn't do it, eventually striking out and giving Britton a big first out and taking some of the Tigers' momentum away.

Still, though, Detroit just needed a single to tie the game. That's when Showalter himself made his way to the mound and prepared to roll the dice. The *Washington Post* reported that the skipper gathered six of the Birds on the mound and said a few things. He first told Britton that his two pitches that had been banged for doubles weren't that bad. Then Showalter unveiled his strategy that raised a few eyebrows.

"We're going to walk this guy. The next guy's going to hit into a double play, and we're gonna go home," the *Post* reported Showalter as saying.

The move went against "the book" that so many people like to refer to in baseball. Putting the winning run on base is generally frowned upon. Showalter did that by telling Britton to intentionally walk Nick Castellanos, which put runners at first and second, still with only one out. A double, a single plus an error, or just some other kind of error could have scored both runs and given the Tigers a 3–2 victory and possibly turned the series around. The TBS broadcasting team joked that Showalter rolled "some big fuzzy dice" on that move and talked for several seconds about how unusual it was to put that go-ahead run on base.

But that's what the Orioles did. Showalter knew that as well as the Tigers hit—and they could crush the ball when things were right—they also featured a very thin bench. They knew that Andrew Romine was due up next, but he was batting just .182 in the series, and this kind of pushed Tigers manager Brad Ausmus to pinch-hit Hernan Perez for Romine. Perez had only five big league at-bats all season long, and Showalter apparently felt the move was worth the risk.

"When you put the winning run on base like that, it takes a lot of guts to do that," Duquette told the *Post*. "It clearly told everybody: Buck was playing to win the series, there and then."

On the second pitch to Perez, the pinch-hitter hit a soft grounder to third baseman Ryan Flaherty. That was quickly turned into a 5-4-3 double play, and Showalter's prediction came true.

After the game, Showalter made it very clear that the intentional walk move was not an easy decision to arrive at and oh, yes, there might have been some hesitation there.

"Just needed a little karma, change the way that inning was going," Showalter said after the game. "Had a lot of faith in Zach and there is a lot of factors going on there. I don't know, you guys can judge conventionality. What is it compared to what's been done? I think each situation changes depending on the strength of your players and the strength of their players on a given night."

Showalter brushed off taking too much credit for the move, but it was easy to see how happy the result made him. After first baseman Steve Pearce caught second baseman Jonathan Schoop's throw to lock up the double play and end the game, Showalter gave bench coach John Russell a big bear hug in the Baltimore dugout. Several of the Orioles coaches and Showalter then got together for a clearly emotional hug. And when that ended, Showalter stood at the bottom of the dugout, looking out at his team with a big smile on his face like a proud teacher or parent.

"I'm a ship passing in the night," Showalter said in the press conference afterwards. "This is fun to watch, and believe me, I'm happier than you can imagine. But most of it comes from getting to see the players get what they put into it."

Showalter also wanted to make sure he enjoyed the moment at that point. The Orioles weren't sure if they'd see the Angels or Royals in the next round, but Showalter, a manager often regarded as too much of a taskmaster in his younger days, was going to take pride in what his team had just done.

He even waxed a bit nostalgic afterwards, telling everyone how much joy he wanted to take from this series victory.

"I'm going to have a lot of fun," he said that day. "I'm looking forward to watching our guys and . . . as I've gotten older, you take it in because these times are fleeting. You're going to look back and wish you had paid more attention to those memories. You know what, what do they say, these are the good old days. We'll be talking about these down the road. And I take a lot of mental snapshots. I always try to get in a good position where nobody can block me out when I know one may be coming. So I'm going to take it in. Hopefully I don't get too nostalgic. But you realize how lucky you are and what an honor it is to be here. You do try to remember when you're needed to do something, then you're ready to do it."

Winning that series seemed also to electrify the city of Baltimore. The Orioles last won a playoff series in 1997 when they beat Seattle in the ALDS. The attendance had picked up at Oriole Park throughout the second half of the season and postseason tickets were almost impossible to come by. When the Orioles beat Detroit, 7–6, in a wild comeback victory in Game 2 of that series, the big hit was a three-run pinch-hit double from Delmon Young. The noise in the stadium proved deafening for many in there. Months later, then Orioles pitcher Tommy Hunter said that was the loudest stadium he could ever remember being in. His teammate Nick Markakis also acknowledged the contributions of the fans.

"You know, the fans, they're the reason why we play this game," Markakis said in the postseason. "To go out there in front of your home crowd and to play a game that we love and to get this far, this late in the season, you know, that's what it's all about. It's all about the fans. And ultimately, we are playing to win, but we're playing to win for the fans. They're the ones that put us out there every day and they're the people that make things happen."

Manager Buck Showalter gives out a hug during the on-field celebration after the Orioles clinched the 2014 American League East Division title.

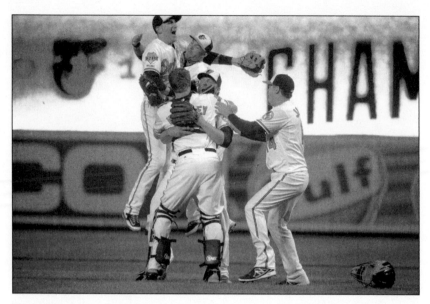

The celebration begins after the Orioles clinched the American League East Division title at home in September 2014.

After the Orioles locked up that series, they appeared to be headed for the World Series. They were set to play Kansas City in the American League Championship Series, a team that most people looked past. The Royals became hot late in the season and made it into the playoffs as a wild-card team. But they then knocked off the A's and Angels in the first two rounds of the playoffs. That certainly raised a few eyebrows, but most experts thought that the ALCS would belong to the Orioles, who were getting all the pitching, hitting, and defense at that time.

This time, though, the experts were wrong. Kansas City's hot streak continued as they swept the Orioles in four close games and moved on to the World Series. The ALCS was one of those series where whatever bad happened seemed to happen to the Orioles, while the Royals seemed to find every good break. Showalter and some of the players said later that every ball they hit either went right at somebody or one of the Kansas City defenders made a great play on it. The Royals made several fabulous plays on defense in the series, doing it time and time again.

The Royals took it to the Orioles throughout the series. They jumped ahead early, posted big innings later and, more than anything else, just took command at the right times. Baltimore was able to gain the lead for just two innings in the entire 37-inning series—from the top of the second until the bottom of the fourth in Game 3 when the Orioles held a 1–0 lead. The Royals won Game 1 with a three-run 10th inning and used a two-run ninth inning to capture Game 2. Both of those outbursts snapped ties and gave the Royals victories in Baltimore and a 2–0 lead in the series.

The Orioles took their first lead of the series early in Game 3 in Kansas City on back-to-back doubles from Pearce and J. J. Hardy. But the Royals chipped their way back against starter Wei-Yin Chen. They got a run in the fourth and took a 2–1 lead in the sixth on a sacrifice fly off Kevin Gausman, who had just come in to relieve Chen, and that's how the game ended.

It was more of the same in Game 4. The Royals scored twice in the first inning on a bizarre play. Kansas City got runners on second and third with no outs off starter Miguel Gonzalez when Eric Hosmer hit a sharp grounder to Steve Pearce at first. Pearce tried to throw home to get lead runner Alcides Escobar. But Escobar got in, and catcher Caleb Joseph could not handle the throw, so it got away. That error let in a second run for a quick 2–0 lead. With the way Kansas City's pitching and defense had performed in the series, that set a bad tone.

The Orioles again could not do much on offense. Kansas City threatened several times but couldn't score again and closed out the series with another 2–1 victory.

What made the Orioles' accomplishments that much more impressive in 2014 involved events that took place off the field. The Orioles lost three All-Star-caliber players to various issues during the year and did not have them for the playoffs. Thus, they needed to rely on the players that Duquette found and Showalter guided to make them a postseason team.

The skipper talked after Game 4 about what his feelings were and how this one hurt, even though it was the first time in seventeen years the team had made it to the American League Championship Series and just one stop from the World Series.

"My emotion is for the players and the organization and the fans, because I keep thinking about something I or we could have done differently," Showalter said. "That's what you think about. But if you care, like our people care, it hurts. And that's why I know how much it hurts those guys. And our fans. They've been there through thick and thin for us in Baltimore. The support of the ownership has been there. Really feel bad about disappointing them, and not be able to get over the hump and roll the dice again."

What the Royals did in the ALCS really took the bat out of Showalter's hands, so to speak. He made so many moves in the ALDS with Detroit, and it seemed like whatever the skipper did worked out. Kansas City used its speed, defensive skills, and ability to manufacture runs to really hurt the Orioles' offense in a number of ways. The Royals took away many hits with their great outfield speed. Their three-man late-inning crew of Kelvin Herrera, Wade Davis, and Greg Holland often shut down the Orioles in the final three or four innings, usually stopping the Baltimore power bats with their power arms.

Also, the Royals manufactured runs on several occasions while the Orioles could not. That was a weakness of the team all season long for Showalter, but Kansas City did it to perfection throughout this series. The Royals stole just one base in the series, but they constantly would race from first to third on a single and take two bases any time they could. It cost the Orioles. When you live by the home run, you'll die by it if you can't hit them and can't manufacture runs.

Chapter Five

THE PREVIOUS LIFE OF BUCK

It's not unusual for a major league manager to have never made it to the big leagues as a player himself. Many times, a great skipper couldn't cut it as well when on the field, which makes it harder in some ways for him as a manager, as players sometimes question how a manager who hasn't played can manage. That, however, is an argument with flaws because managers and coaches who weren't as good themselves often can be better at this job since they needed to work harder at their baseball skills than superstars with natural talent. They understand more. They can empathize more.

Longtime manager Earl Weaver was one of those. He hit pretty well in the minor leagues but never could make it to the majors. But when he took over as the manager of the Orioles at the 1968 All-Star break, Weaver knew how to handle the team and the game. That's why he eventually became a member of the Hall of Fame. The similarities between Weaver and Show-alter are very interesting—perhaps the most glaring of which is they didn't play in the majors but did just fine managing there.

Their situations weren't as similar when they took over the teams. When Weaver got the job, the Orioles had won the

World Series just two years before and stumbled after that. They couldn't seem to return to that level of play, which is why then-GM Harry Dalton offered Weaver the job midway through a 1968 season that saw the Detroit Tigers running away with the American League title (there were no divisions at that point). Weaver joked about how fortunate he was to find a very talented roster waiting at his disposal, with big-time players like Brooks and Frank Robinson, Jim Palmer, Boog Powell, and others. He talked about that at the ceremony where the Orioles revealed the statue of the skipper at Oriole Park at Camden Yards.

"If they weren't there, I probably wouldn't be here," Weaver said that day. "I had some pretty good ballplayers."

Despite the different situations in which they found themselves upon their arrival in Baltimore, the two held very similar views. They wanted perfection and didn't like mistakes, especially when it came to fundamentals. Hit the cut-off man, move the runner up, don't make errors, make the right plays. These types of plays were something the Orioles simply did not do during their 14 straight losing seasons (1998–2011).

The way Weaver drilled his team and players so hard is something that really made an impression on Showalter.

"He just never gave in," Showalter said. "Never. I think because of how he got where he got, he was not going to leave any stone unturned. He didn't want to let people down. He was . . . [constantly] striving for perfection in an imperfect game."

That's a battle all managers must fight, of course. It's something that can be tougher for managers who might have to prove themselves in a different way. It did not take long for Weaver to prove his skills, however, despite not playing in the major leagues because the Orioles won 109 games in his first full season and earned a trip to the World Series. But Weaver had taken charge of a team with plenty of talent on the roster, whereas Showalter came to a team that really did not have very much.

That's why fundamentals and doing the little things right probably mean so much to Buck Showalter, particularly in those early days with the Orioles. He understood what it took to find success and wanted his players also to grasp that concept.

"He grinded it out through the minor leagues both a player and a manager and a coach. He worked his way up, and he was . . . this [wunderkind] manager. When you take over the Yankees at 36 and start doing things there and then having success. I think it probably earns you some success moving forward," said WBAL sports broadcaster Brett Hollander. "The difference was pretty palpable, I think, at first. I had seen a lot of managers come and go, front office types come and go. And although looking at that team in 2010, there was a fair amount of talent there, a lot of first-round picks that had either gotten there or were going to get there soon. They had a great finish in that 2010 season so immediately you thought there was a chance that this guy was special, and that he could make an instant difference."

Showalter was picked by the Yankees in the 1977 draft after setting a school record at Mississippi State with a .459 batting average—that remains the team's standard. He also had been an All-American at Chipola Junior College (Marianna, Florida). Showalter played in the New York minor-league system as a first baseman and outfielder from 1977–83 and posted a .294 average.

Showalter became a very strong hitter. He even finished first in the Double-A Southern League with 178 hits in 1980, the year Showalter ended up second in the league with a .324 average. Nashville won a league-record 97 games that season.

But Showalter then ran into trouble when prospect Don Mattingly began to find his way, also at first base. Showalter has joked several times over the years that when he saw Mattingly play, he knew his path to the major leagues would become harder. In fact, Showalter did make it to Triple-A eventually, playing part of two seasons there, but never getting any higher or reaching the majors.

After that, Showalter stayed with the Yankees and began coaching in the minor leagues. He started managing in 1985 and did that job through 1989 with three different teams in three different leagues and wound up with four first-place finishes in five years. That's when Showalter made the big leagues, starting as a coach with New York in 1990 and eventually moving up to become the manager in 1992, just before his 36th birthday. The Yankees were in the process of rebuilding their farm system and were just about to really take off; Showalter guided the young players well.

Showalter posted a record of 313–268 in four seasons with the Yankees and helped the team to a playoff appearance in 1995. That's when his time with New York ended due to a disagreement with management over firing some coaches. He then landed with Arizona and managed that team for the first three years before getting fired after the 2000 season. Texas was his next stop, and Showalter managed there from 2003–2006.

So it had been a while since Showalter managed a major league team when he took over the Orioles for the final two months of 2010. But still, Showalter knew what he wanted to do, and the team pretty much agreed with it. This was not an easy task because of the Orioles' 32–73 record when Showalter took over. He faced a difficult task in many ways but was determined to change the way the Orioles did things. They had run through several managers and front-office personnel. It truly was time to turn things around, and Showalter knew what he had to do.

"Getting the players to buy in and be accountable to the manager and one another, that has been, I think, Buck's greatest asset. Even with that, it takes time," said WBAL sports broadcaster Pete Gilbert. "In 2011, [his first full season] they only won 69 games. In 2012, they come back and the account-ability is there. Adam Jones . . . signed because of Buck. He saw what was happening. He saw the culture change. He saw the idea that we're going to do things the right way, and if you're not going to do them this way, you're not going to be here, plain and simple. Even if Dave Trembley had said that, he didn't have the authority to back it up. He didn't have the credentials to back it up. He hadn't built winners elsewhere in which the players believed."

Gilbert talked about the fact that even though Showal-ter never played in the major leagues, his record of success preceded him, something the players clearly understood and respected. While other managers had lost the clubhouse, Showalter gained control over it and made his moves.

"The difference is the track record," Gilbert said. "Buck had won in New York. Buck had won in Arizona. Buck had won in Texas. When you talk to him, what I so much like about him is he clearly is the smartest guy in the room, but he lets you know that in a non-insulting way."

The Orioles wanted to make a bold move when hiring Showalter, but it took a little while for everything to fall into place. They spent much of that summer looking for a new skipper and had even offered the job to Bobby Valentine before settling on Showalter. At that time, Andy MacPhail was the team's president of baseball operations, and he harbored some real concerns about the direction the club was heading.

"What we have currently in our franchise is we have a young core of players struggling, taking a step backwards," MacPhail said at Showalter's introductory press conference in 2010. "They haven't been exposed to a winning type environment. We, for the past couple of months, have been trying to find somebody that has had some experience in creating that environment, [and has been] exposed to young

rosters. He's done it in three different places. We need somebody that can put his stamp on the team and have us play a
certain brand of baseball that we're going to have to play to
win. He has a reputation that excels or equals all others in
that category."

Showalter made it clear that even though Baltimore had
plenty of excuses—the Yankees spent more money, as did the
Red Sox, Tampa Bay was now a contender, and Toronto kept
improving. The Orioles were in the American League East.
Period. So they needed to, instead of complaining about who
they'd be batting, find a way to beat them.

"The bottom line is, are you doing something on that field
as an organization and as a team that people want to sell their
soul to and feel comfortable about trusting that players are
going to give effort, players are going to be sincere about what
they're doing and the way they go about it? Some people
don't like that accountability, and we'll sort that out," Showalter said at that introductory press conference. "You hear people
talk about realignment. I don't really care. The Yankees aren't
going away, the Red Sox aren't going away, and Tampa's not
going away. And Toronto's getting better. You've got to figure
out a way to do it."

Showalter's record of success spoke for him, although so
did his reputation as someone overly focused on the details
who wanted to have his hand in just about everything. The
players knew that. In fact, those who worked with Showalter
at various points in his first three jobs said that became his
Achilles' heel.

When Bob Brenly took over as the Arizona manager in
2001 after Showalter was let go after helping the franchise
make the playoffs very quickly, the new skipper wanted to let
his team know things would not be as tight around the ballpark.
He kind of borrowed from what John Madden often told his
team when coaching the Oakland Raiders from 1968–1978.

Buck Showalter spends much of his pre-game time looking around the field to see what's going on with both teams.

Madden said he wouldn't bother his team with a lot of rules, except two: be on time and play like hell.

That's the message Brenly tried to give the Diamondbacks when he took over in the spring of 2001. According to a *New York Times* article, Brenly reportedly threw a book in the trash can in front of the players and told them that life would be different that season. His comments emphasized the contrast between the two managerial styles.

"It was a player development manual, a big, thick, heavy ring-binder notebook," Brenly said in the article. "I just dropped it on the ground. I had a cocktail napkin in my back pocket. I pulled it out and I said: 'These were the rules last year; these are the rules this year. Be on time and get the job done.' It was more a theatrical thing than anything else. I just felt in my first meeting as manager in front of the team, you wanted them to understand we were going to be loose and we were going to have fun, and I expected them to conduct themselves like professionals but at the same time have a little fun, relax and enjoy what we do for a living. Hopefully that helped drive it home right away."

Meanwhile, Showalter, in his first year in Baltimore, faced a bit of a multi-faceted task due to the poor recent history of Baltimore baseball. Since the city hadn't found success in baseball since 1997, interest in the franchise had severely waned. The move of the Montreal Expos to Washington in 2005, which created competition between the two teams for local fans, also did not help matters. But fourteen straight losing seasons makes it hard for fans to keep coming out. Plus, when the Yankees or Red Sox came to Baltimore, they brought loads of fans that made it seem kind of like a road game for the Orioles.

That's what turning around the franchise could do. The Orioles couldn't really expect to immediately return to the level of their glory years in the '60s and '70s when they made the World Series four times in six years and won twice. Becoming a winning and competitive team was really the first goal, and it's a change that Showalter played a major role in.

"He's done something for my generation that's more important than any one single World Series victory," Hollander said in a July 2015 interview. "He's made baseball relevant and matter again. He made it matter with the current youth of Baltimore, which is more important than any one single World Series victory and then, also, an older generation that kind of lost interest in it. They seem fully invested again."

Chapter Six

THE DEFENDER

Fans greeted Orioles first baseman Chris Davis with cheers upon his return to Camden Yards for the team's home opener on April 10, 2015. If there were any hard feelings about his twenty-five-game suspension for violating the league's policy on banned substances, the home crowd did a nice job hiding those emotions. Because of the suspension, Davis missed the Orioles' entire postseason run in 2014. Davis was apologetic throughout the ordeal and there were some questions about how well he would be received by the home fans. The applause seemed to vindicate him a bit. However, the cheers seemed to diminish throughout the game, as he went hitless in four at-bats.

Showalter did not appear to have any animosity toward Davis for the indiscretion. However, Showalter rarely, if ever, calls out a player while speaking to the media. Part of his strengths as a leader is he doesn't ever try to embarrass a player or criticize them publicly. Behind closed doors, Showalter has no problem discussing potential issues or problems with a player individually.

"I don't try to beat him up on some things that are pretty obvious," Showalter said. "I don't say, 'Hey, how are you feeling?'

or 'How's that going to be?' Like I said, Chris had 209 days without playing a major league game. I'm trying to let him kind of sort his way through it. A lot of new things going on."

Showalter is savvy at balancing the need to protect his players while understanding how the paying customer can become frustrated. That skill can be found in all of the game's most effective managers. It creates an ethos where the fans and players trust the man in charge. Chris Davis underscored this challenge. Davis knew he made a big mistake. Showalter and the fellow players didn't need to remind him of it everyday. In the end, the fans were just as forgiving.

"There are a lot of emotional challenges and he'll be the first to tell you that some of them were self-inflicted, but you've got to fight your way through them," Showalter said about the slugger.

Showalter is generally one of the most media-friendly managers in the game, and even in his discussion of Davis and the suspension, he didn't shy away from reporters. He often spends much of his pre-game manager's meeting with reporters to talk football, movies or current events. He remains patient with questions he's already answered a dozen times. One of the challenges for any manager is the access media is allowed and how much he must spend dealing with their inquiries. Yet he didn't once back away from dealing with questions about Davis and how it was affecting the team. Showalter simply reminded the media that he was in charge and one issue was not going to derail the team or the season.

However, who would have blamed Showalter had he held a grudge or decided to further discipline Davis for the infraction? Davis was suspended September 12, 2014, for testing positive for amphetamines associated with Adderall—a substance banned by MLB. It was Davis's second violation and his 25-game suspension took effect immediately. This meant he would miss the remaining 17 games of the regular season and

*Manager Buck Showalter and first baseman Chris Davis watch during a game. Showalter
stood behind Davis even when he was struggling during the first part of 2015.*

as many as eight playoffs games if the Orioles were to advance
that far in the postseason.

At the time of the suspension, the Orioles were rolling with
a 10-game lead in the AL East. But to fans, there were
questions about whether the team could hold onto its first-
place position, especially with All-Stars Manny Machado and
Matt Wieters each out for the season with knee and elbow
injuries, respectively.

Showalter, who got the news while watching the Ravens'
Thursday night game against the Steelers, remained even-
keeled as he faced a throng of media. There was no sense of
panic despite dealing with so much adversity.

"I'm disappointed," Showalter said. "I know Chris is, too,
but it is what it is. We'll try to deal with it and move on.
Timing's never good, but it's one of those challenges. It's why
we have [testing] in place. Fully supportive of it. These are the
things that everybody knew about beforehand, and it's another
way that we want our fans to be able to trust a lot of things."

Much like many NFL coaches, Showalter developed a "next man up" mentality. Dan Duquette, the Orioles executive vice president, baseball operations, had picked up Kelly Johnson, who could serve as a stop-gap, in a trade with Boston in late August. Steve Pearce also had a solid year and was a viable substitute for Davis at first base.

"I've got a lot of confidence in our guys," Showalter said. "We're always looking at the what-ifs. Chris has had some physical issues and we've been able to plug some people in that did a nice job for us, so we'll see."

Outfielder Travis Snider, who came to the Orioles for the 2015 season via a trade with the Pirates, also got some early experience with Showalter's leadership style. Snider misplayed a liner by Toronto's Devon Travis on April 12 that cost Baltimore three runs in a 10–7 loss. Snider later hit a three-run homer to get the Orioles back in the game.

After the game, Showalter chose to highlight the positive impact Snider made to the club, rather than his defensive gaffe.

"He did some good things," Showalter said. "He hit a three-run homer that got us back in the ballgame. He made a play where the wind blew the ball back in that a lot of guys may not have made. Travis is considered a good outfielder and today he got a tough read on one ball. He's already made two or three plays. He actually won a game for us defensively in Tampa just about, so just one of those things. He's a good outfielder."

It also helped that Snider, who did not last the entire season with the Orioles, took full responsibility for his mistake. The Orioles under Showalter have been an accountable group. When a starter fails to go deep into a game, he is often waiting at his locker for post-game questions. He does not leave the ballpark early. A reliever who gave up a costly home run would often explain how he made the mistake. Hitters in slumps? Fire away. That cultivated a transparent clubhouse where there was rarely the tension that came with a decade of losing under previous managers.

Early in the 2015 season, the Orioles' beleaguered bullpen allowed at least a run over the first 10 games. Brad Brach was one of the relievers who struggled early. Brach threw two scoreless innings in early an April game against the Yankees just three days after struggling against the Blue Jays.

His manager had his back the entire time.

"Brad's a very versatile pitcher," Showalter said. "On a given night he can do just about anything you want to do with him. Give you multiple innings here and there or pitch a meaningful eighth if somebody needs a day. I like the way he defends himself against left-hand hitters with the change-up."

Tommy Hunter was another reliever who struggled mightily in the early part of the 2015 season. The low point was allowing a go-ahead grand slam to Yankees pinch hitter Stephen Drew on April 13. He had allowed six runs in four appearances (3.2) for a 14.73 ERA at that point of the season.

If Showalter was concerned, he certainly didn't tip his hand to the media.

"Tommy's got so much, I don't know, loose energy," Showalter said. "He wants to contribute so bad he kind of gets out of whack a little bit. Gets into overthrow mode. It's hard to back him off. Got a big strikeout of Rodriguez. He'll be better. His track record says he'll go through some bumps and you'll like him when it's all said and done."

Showalter's attitude and team-first concept was contagious for the players. Brach came to his fellow relievers' defense.

"The only pressure that we have is on ourselves, and really we're not pressing yet. It's the first week. It hasn't been the best, but it's seven games in, eight games in, nine games in. There's nothing really to panic about, so really there's no pressure. I just want to go out and put up a zero like I always do."

Buck Showalter isn't quite as fiery as he used to be, but the Orioles' skipper still won't hesitate to let an umpire know his feelings.

By the end of May, Baltimore's bullpen was one of the best in MLB. The Orioles' relievers went 6–1 with a 2.40 ERA over 82 2/3 innings. They also struck out 87 batters with just 25 walks.

However, Showalter's defense of his players extended beyond the media. If there was an issue with an umpire, Showalter swooped down to help his players. On April 17, 2015, against the Red Sox, Orioles starter Ubaldo Jimenez was ejected for hitting Pablo Sandoval in the right shoulder in the fourth inning. At the time, Jimenez had not even allowed a hit.

Home plate umpire Jordan Baker did not issue a warning before the ejection and appeared to jump to the conclusion that Jimenez hit a batter on purpose. This prompted Showalter to leap from the dugout and defend Jimenez, who is not known for hitting opposing players.

Showalter did not get ejected, but after the game he was still steaming from the incident.

"Quite contrary to what people think, every time some-body gets hit [with a pitch] it's not intentional," Showalter said. "And we applaud anybody sliding hard or playing the game right. It's just unfortunate that something like that gets involved in the game and now it really sets our bullpen with some challenges. I'm hoping that MLB will take the proper steps to make sure they know that was incorrect. It was pretty obvious to everybody."

There was speculation that Jimenez was retaliating against Sandoval for his hard slide into Orioles second baseman Jona-than Schoop in the second inning. That theory also did not sit well with Showalter. He had instilled a sense of ethics among his team and did not appreciate when people questioned that philosophy. He quickly put the onus back on the umpire.

"I guess [Baker's] thinking that someone's mad about somebody sliding hard," Showalter said. "I mean, we all aspire to play the game that way. It's quite frankly professionally embarrassing. What it does [to] your whole bullpen for the rest of the trip, I mean we had to use people we wouldn't normally use."

That wasn't the only confrontation the Orioles had to deal with in the early part of the 2015 season. Another involved Toronto outfielder Jose Bautista. First, Bautista took exception to an inside pitch by Darren O'Day on April 12. He then homered later in the at-bat and appeared to taunt O'Day as he ran around the bases.

After the game, Bautista claimed O'Day has a history of throwing at him. The two players do have a tumultuous his-tory. Bautista claims O'Day has been throwing at him since 2013, which the right-hander has continuously dismissed.

"This is the only guy that this happens with in the whole league," Bautista said. "I don't have any history with anybody. The reason I have a history with this guy is on one particular thing. I don't know what day of the week it was, he struck me out and he started yapping at me. After that it's been a back and forth of emotional situations."

Just over a week later, tempers flared again. This time, Bautista directed his anger at rookie pitcher Jason Garcia after the twenty-two-year old also threw inside to him in the seventh inning. Three pitches later, Bautista had the last word again with a home run, admiring the flight of the ball before he rounded the bases.

Showalter did not openly criticize Bautista. However, his players took exception, especially center fielder Adam Jones, who yelled something to Bautista coming off the field and then went on the record after the game.

"It's not his first, it's not a walk-off, it's in the seventh inning," Jones said. "Let's not walk halfway down the line. Respect the game. I know he does, but at that moment right there he didn't, and when it happens against my team, I'm going to take offense to it."

Perhaps Showalter was less focused on Bautista's antics than concern over his team's performance in the first month of the season. Starter Bud Norris was one of several starters who struggled early on. Norris lost his first two starts and had an ERA of 17.42. Again, Showalter showed faith in his player.

"Command has been an issue for him, getting the ball where he needs to get it consistently and it's a situation where his track record says he's better than that," Showalter said. "We'll trust that."

Good teams stand behind one another. That philosophy has been evident since Showalter became manager of the Orioles in 2010 and almost instantaneously turned the moribund franchise into a winner. The city was once again aglow in Orange. Fans even wore T-shirts with Showalter's image or one of his catch-phrases, "I like our guys."

People generally respond to a true leader and Showalter had the charisma. It also didn't hurt that he was finding success with the Orioles years after he led the rival Yankees. The manager's success was a badge of honor for a city that often never feels like it is good enough. Many Baltimore residents always feel like they are living in the shadows of bigger cities like Washington, DC, Philadelphia, and New York. The city embraces any opportunity to stand out.

This was one of the main reasons they embraced their successful Major League Baseball manager.

In his return, Showalter not only defends his players, but stands up for the entire City of Baltimore. And when the losing starts as it inevitably does through the course of a long Major League Baseball season, it is just not effective leadership to start pointing fingers. Following three straight losses to the Astros on June 3, 2015, Showalter could sense the frustration from the players and fans as the team fell a season-worst six games under .500.

But he stood strong.

"It's very easy to start beating up on people," Showalter said. "I'm certainly not going to. We do a lot of things behind the scenes. We grind it. This is a challenging time. This too shall pass but you wanted it to happen yesterday."

While voicing some concern, Showalter remained publicly confident in his team. When he took the job with the Orioles in 2010, he inherited a club with more than a decade of losing seasons. An early season slump was just a hiccup compared to the challenge of changing the entire culture of an organization.

"We'll continue to look at ways to get better. It's a challenging time for everybody but it'll make us stronger in the long run. We need to figure it out very soon."

Chapter Seven
THE BULLPEN SHUFFLE

Managing a pitching staff is one of the biggest challenges for a manager. Not only do managers have to carefully define roles, but also they have to be delicate when relief pitchers fail or they lose their spot to an emerging arm in the minors. Starting pitchers who struggle are often relegated to the bullpen to work on their mechanics. Some thrive and some pout over this new role. Managers have to be able to bring it all together for the sake of the team.

Showalter has proven himself to be a master of that craft. Under his direction, the Orioles have developed one of the strongest bullpens in Major League Baseball. The players have changed, but the positive results have ostensibly remained the same. Showalter has found a way to find the right balance among his staff.

No position is trickier than closer. These are the pitchers that are expected to throw an inning and secure a victory. Obviously, it's not as easy as it sounds and things do not always go as planned. Few players embody this challenge more than former Orioles closer Jim Johnson, who forced Showalter to make several tough decisions on the job. For a couple of seasons, the Orioles had one of the best closers in the game with Johnson. He was especially valuable to the Orioles because he was a home-grown talent, having been drafted in the fifth round of the 2011 MLB Draft.

Johnson was originally slotted to be a starter. However, the Orioles needed an extra arm out of the bullpen and he was promoted from Triple-A Norfolk on April 12, 2008, to fill that need. Johnson wound up thriving in that role, and at one point, he threw 18 straight scoreless innings. Later that season, Johnson was given the opportunity to serve as closer when George Sherrill was forced onto the disabled list with inflammation in his left shoulder. Johnson finished the 2008 season with a 2.23 ERA in 54 appearances (68.2 innings) with one save.

One year later, Johnson was named the full-time closer when Sherrill was sent to the Dodgers at the trade deadline. While he finished with 10 saves in 2009 on a struggling team, injury issues and other pitchers kept Johnson out of the clos-er's role until 2012.

Prior to the 2012 season, Johnson signed a one-year, $2.6 million with the Orioles to avoid arbitration. This decision paid huge dividends for Baltimore because Johnson wound up leading the league with 51 saves in 2012. He was named to the American League All-Star team and won the esteemed AL Rolaids Relief Man Award. When Johnson reached the 50-save plateau on September 30, Showalter was quick to praise the right-hander and the confidence he brought to the team.

"You have no idea how I respect that accomplishment," Showalter told reporters about the 50 saves. "I've been right there with every one of them. It's been an honor to watch, the whole process of him as a pitcher, a teammate, a man."

While Johnson had solid numbers in the 2013 season when he led the American League with 50 saves, he wasn't quite as dominant as he'd been the year before. One of the glaring issues was blowing nine of his 59 save opportunities. This put Baltimore in a difficult position when the season ended because Johnson was eligible to make more than $10 million in 2014 through arbitration. Instead of allocating all of that money for a closer, the Orioles decided to trade Johnson to Oakland for second baseman Jemile Weeks and a minor leaguer.

This would provide another challenge for Showalter to find a new pitcher to play such a pivotal role. Showalter was once again unflappable in the face of potential adversity. He took the news in stride and expressed confidence in finding a new closer within the organization.

"There are some other guys that might step up, having a year under their belt they hadn't before," Showalter said at the winter meetings later that month. "Let's face it, chemistry comes from winning games, to start off with. You can start with good chemistry out in the spring. But if you go 0–30 in April, I bet your chemistry isn't real good. It runs hand in hand."

Showalter went into 2014 spring training with an open mind and a sharp eye for a potential closer. Tommy Hunter, Darren O'Day, and Ryan Webb emerged as the top candidates, but none of them had previously served in that role. Hunter was the early pick because he threw hard and had the steely mentality to close out a game. Showalter, however, refused to tip his hand.

"Obviously, Tommy's a strong candidate," Showalter told reporters at the team's spring training facility in Sarasota, Florida. "I'm not going to handicap this every day. I don't mind doing this every day. I don't think it's productive for the players."

The players also were not taking anything for granted. They knew Showalter would be scrutinizing the position closely. The new closer, whoever he wound up being, would have to earn it. That didn't just mean performing well in games. It meant an all-around solid performance and perfecting every nuance demanded by the manager.

"It's up in the air right now for everyone, so we'll see what happens," Hunter said. "Buck likes those challenges during spring. What are they, competitions? Challenges? Those competitions come out and play. We'll see what happens."

Hunter did indeed win the job as closer heading into Opening Day in 2014. He started strong by converting 11 save opportunities. However, Hunter blew two save chances on May 10 against Houston and May 13 against the Tigers. He was then forced to the disabled list with a left groin strain. In his absence, Zach Britton, a former starter, took over as closer, picked up his first career save on May 15, and never relinquished the role. Even when Hunter returned, he was back in the bullpen as a setup man.

Replacing a closer is a tough decision for any manager. But Showalter knew he had to do what was best for the club. In this case, he liked what he saw from Britton, who had previously dealt with some confidence issues with some struggles as a starter. Britton had the necessary mechanics to be the difference as the last guy out of the bullpen as well as a dynamic hard sinker that batters often couldn't touch.

"We're going to use whatever gives us the best chance to win, the best chance to put guys in the best spot to be successful and to be healthy," Showalter said. "That's the way we are looking at it."

Britton finished the 2014 season by converting 37 of the 41 save chances. He also had a 1.65 ERA, playing a vital role in the Orioles' postseason run that season. Britton responded the Showalter's trust in him to close out a game. Most importantly, he embraced his new role and this allowed him to thrive. By 2015, he was one of the top closers in all of Major League Baseball and was named to his first All-Star team.

"It's crazy. It's funny how things work, baseball works," Britton said near the end of the 2014 season. "You go from one year unsure about how your career is going to unfold with some injuries and not feeling like I was 100 percent to having a good off-season and coming back and just regaining confidence," Britton said. "To be in a position where I'm closing games out for these guys, it's special, something I didn't expect going into this year. And if someone would have told me, I would have laughed it off as a joke."

But it was no joke. Showalter is a top evaluator of talent and he saw a winner with Britton. Managing the rest of the bullpen posed a different challenge. Some relievers have to be able to throw multiple innings if the starter struggles. This also takes him out of the equation to pitch for the next couple of days because the reliever will need some rest. Showalter is a huge proponent of not overworking his pitchers. In addition to managing the various arms, a baseball manager also has to be cognizant of the delicate egos of some pitchers. Some of them simply don't respond as well as others in terms of adversity. Dealing with pitchers has to be done on an individual basis because of the different personalities.

Ubaldo Jimenez presented one of the biggest challenges in 2014 just after he signed a four-year $50 million deal with the club, which was the largest in team history for a free-agent pitcher. Jimenez was expected to anchor the rotation, but instead, he struggled from almost the very beginning. He especially struggled with his command, allowing too many base-runners via walks.

Jimenez also had some hard luck in his first season with the Orioles. He was forced to the DL in July because of an ankle sprain suffered in the parking lot outside of his Baltimore apartment. After going 4–9 with a 4.83 ERA through the first four months of the season, Showalter sent him to the bullpen on August 19. Jimenez took the demotion in stride and Showalter did his best to try and get him back on track by limiting his innings, and consequently, limiting the damage. It was a gutsy call for the manager to drop his highest-paid pitcher out of the rotation.

"We don't have any limitations now on anybody, so there'll be a need that Ubaldo can serve this team," Showalter said. "It could be as a starter, and it could be as a reliever, but right now, for the next five games six [days], we know where we're going."

Jimenez, however, could not quite get fully back on track. With the postseason looming, Showalter was faced with more tough roster decisions. He decided to retain Jimenez for the ALDS against the Tigers, but he did not pitch. Showalter then dropped the right-hander for the ALCS against Kansas City, opting instead for left-hander Brian Matusz.

Showalter, however, was never publicly critical of Jimenez. The skipper also expressed confidence that Jimenez would eventually turn things around. That confidence was rewarded in the 2015 season when Jimenez tweaked his mechanics and became the top starter in the rotation, earning the first start for the team following the All-Star break. Jimenez had a simple explanation for his turnaround.

"The command of the fastball," Jimenez said. "That's the number one thing for every starter. Especially for me, throughout my career it's been difficult to have good mechanics and command the fastball. I've had to deal with a lot of walks, a lot of command issues. That's the thing I'm really proud of."

Showalter also felt vindicated by Jimenez's resurgence. It was also a lesson to other managers about the importance of patience. Showalter and the club knew Jimenez had talent and that's the reason they offered him the big contract. Both the pitcher and his coaches worked through the difficulties to find solutions. Showalter could not have been happier with the outcome.

"He's not ever going to take anything for granted," Show-alter said. "He's been going at it since the last pitch he threw last year, really. We felt like it was there. We'll see what the season takes. I feel great for him. He was a welcome addition. Once again, he pitched some good games for us last year in big spots."

Chapter Eight
BUCK ON THE OFFENSIVE

Showalter caused a stir on August 1, 2013 when his comments appeared in *USA Today* about the Yankees and the potential fallout with the suspension of third baseman/DH Alex Rodriguez. Showalter was not too happy about the Yankees possibly not having to pay A-Rod's $25 million salary in 2014 if he was suspended for the entire season. That scenario would have allowed the Yankees to get below the $189 million luxury tax threshold and free up a significant amount of money.

Such a scenario could have implications for teams like Baltimore, and as a result Showalter implored then-Commissioner Bud Selig to take appropriate action. It was simply not fair for the Yankees to benefit financially from A-Rod's transgressions.

In comments to *USA Today* that went viral, Showalter said, "If Bud lets them get away with that, they're under the luxury tax. If they can reset, they can spend again, and I guarantee you in two years Matt Wieters is in New York."

After the comments appeared, Showalter faced several questions prior to the team's game against the Astros on August

1. Showalter told the media that the conversation with the *USA Today* reporter was off-the-record. The comments, however, were printed and in the new world of "be-first, be-fast," the quote immediately circulated to most major sports media outlets in the country.

"It wasn't meant for public consumption," Showalter said to the media prior to the game against the Astros. "You guys know, we sit around and we talk all the time about baseball issues because we kind of love our game. We look at things and talk about it. Unfortunately, somebody decided to put it out there publicly. I said it, and someone decided to print it. It's unfortunate, what are you going to do?"

Wieters was one of the leaders of the clubhouse throughout the season. He wanted no part of being dragged into the controversy. He took the high-road with the local media.

"I'm happy to be here right now, and I'm not thinking about where I'm going to be playing in two years, that's for sure," Wieters said.

Instead of having the controversial comments loom over the team, Showalter used it as a broader opportunity to look at the broader controversy with regard to the Biogenesis case. Showalter said the issue cast a pall over the game and it would take some time to win back the trust of some of the fans.

"I don't think there's going to be some magical date where we can say this is behind us," he said. "If you compare it to society, we're ahead of the curve, but we're not normal society. Our curve's gotta be different. It's gotta be 100 percent."

Showalter also used the issue to point out that his current team largely avoided being part of the scandal. He also used the opportunity to laud his team for playing the game the right way. Showalter said the Orioles players were also looking forward to MLB moving past everything related to the Biogenesis scandal.

"I can tell you in our locker room, I can't speak for other ones but I think it's the case [elsewhere], the common denominator is that they welcome this," Showalter said. "I know talking to our players, it's not like they're ready for it to be over, they're ready because it kind of soils all of them in their mind."

It was not the first or last time Showalter would tackle some of the bigger issues facing the game. When instant replay was introduced prior to the 2014 season, it rankled the feathers of some of baseball's traditionalists. Nonetheless, all 30 clubs unanimously approved the proposal for instant replay. Showalter was an advocate for the new system. He said the new replay system was going to help the game and relieve some of the pressure off the umpires. Ultimately, though, replay was going to allow the correct call to be made . . . at least most of the time.

"The bottom line, it's going to make our game better," Showalter said at the MLB Winter Meetings in December 2013. "I think it's going to be a little bit of an entertainment factor for the fans. Can you imagine watching the NFL or a college game without replay now? I think after a year or so, we're going to say, 'Why did we wait so long?'"

Showalter cautioned there were going to be some glitches with the system. Furthermore, he cautioned that questions would arise, such as where to place runners in certain situations, but in the end, the game was "going to be better." He was also optimistic the system would improve each season as the administration of MLB and the managers continue to work out some of the challenges related to the new system.

As a former basketball referee, Showalter fully understood the challenges facing game officials and the pressure to make the correct call. That experience helped him understand the merits of the system.

"It's a step in the right direction," Showalter said. "The umpires care so much about getting it right. I think this helps

them . . . that's an educated guess. It's the hardest game to offi-
ciate and now we've made it easier."

While there have been ups and downs with the replay system, few can argue how it has helped improve the game. MLB
has even done an effective job speeding up the process. A typical review of a play is usually much shorter than the time it
took for a manager to argue a call with an umpire, making the
game a bit less contentious.

For the 2015 season, Major League Baseball tried to put
more effort into speeding up the game after getting feedback
from fans that the game was simply too long. MLB games
took an average of three hours and two minutes in 2014,
meaning the final out occurred just after 10:00 p.m. EST
on weekdays at most stadiums. One change MLB mandated
was that all batters must keep at least one foot in the batter's
box. There was some leeway with timeouts and wild pitchers.
Timers were also used to keep the game moving, especially
with a pitching change.

Again, Showalter stayed progressive and was open to the
changes that would help speed up the game.

"I'm in support of anything that enhances our game,"
Showalter said. "There are people who have been studying it
and looking at it a lot more intently than we have. I personally
don't think a lot about that part of it, but people smarter than
me that have researched it a lot more than me think it's something we need to do, so I'm in support of that."

Chapter Nine

THE PROTESTS

On April 12, 2015, a twenty-five-year-old African American named Freddie Gray was approached by police for suspicious activity in West Baltimore at 8:39 a.m. Almost an hour later, Gray died in police custody. The lack of details and murky circumstances surrounding the death infuriated local residents. The issue continued to simmer and residents demanded that the police officers involved in the arrest be charged with a crime. This set off a chain of events like no other in the history of Baltimore as people continued to demand answers that were not forthcoming.

Tensions finally boiled over on Saturday, April 25, a few hours prior to the Orioles game against the Red Sox. What was supposed to be a peaceful protest quickly escalated into violence around Baltimore's most popular tourist destination, Harborplace. Police cars were vandalized, store fronts were shattered, and protesters eventually gathered outside Camden Yards and continued to throw objects at law enforcement officials. Tension filled the air as fans tried to enter Camden Yards amid the violence and uncertainty.

Showalter initially was not around for any of the distur-
bances because he had flown to Nashville, Tennessee, to attend
a memorial service for his father-in-law, He eventually made
it back in the dugout by the third inning, but the travel was
challenging because of the unrest and the fact that downtown
was being sealed off by the Baltimore police. Showalter was
kept up-to-date in the interim, on both the developments
throughout the game as well as the ongoing safety concerns.
It was an all-around stressful day for the manager and the city.

"I was aware. Kevin Buck, our traveling secretary, picked
me up at the airport and there was some question whether
we'd be able to get in," Showalter said. "Obviously, the team's
in great hands with [bench coach] John [Russell] and the staff
and the players more importantly. Obviously, attentions were
elsewhere for most of the day, but when I landed he brought
me up to speed on some things."

The game had started at the regularly scheduled 7:05 p.m.
time, but it was a surreal scene as police helicopters hovered
above the stadium throughout the game and tension filled the
air. While the baseball media and fans focused on the game,
local news stations followed the unrest live outside the stadium. Orioles closer Zach Britton entered in the ninth with
a one-run lead, but immediately loaded the bases with one
out on a walk and two singles. Then, the usually sure-handed
Orioles third baseman Manny Machado committed a throwing error on a grounder by Pablo Sandoval and the game was
tied at three. It was a perfect storm for the Orioles literally and
figuratively.

At that point, a light rain began to fall and the Orioles
announced that no one was permitted to leave the stadium
because of the escalating rioting throughout the night. On
the diamond, Boston took the lead in the 10th when Xander
Bogaerts led off with a home run off Baltimore right-hander
Brad Brach. This only added to the already palpable tension

at Camden Yards. The Orioles, however, responded with their most exciting comeback of the young season.

Adam Jones led off in the bottom half of the inning with a triple off former teammate Koji Uehara. Davis then tied the game on a long sacrifice fly. David Lough, who began the season injured and played sparingly, solidified the 5–4 victory with a towering home run to right field. A horde of Orioles players eager to celebrate the stunning victory met Lough at the plate. It was also a nice distraction for the fans, who didn't even know when they were going to be able to leave the stadium. Eventually, police were able to get enough of a handle on the situation where fans were allowed to leave via a detour out of the city. The players' exuberance, however, was muted as they and Showalter took some time to reflect on the unrest growing around Baltimore.

"There's a lot of things going on around our city," Showalter told the media. "And rightfully so, your mind wanders some. We're all human beings. Really proud. Adam [Jones] just keeps grinding through things. What a leader he is. He's been impressive. But he's that way when he's 0-for-15, so that's what's even doubly impressive. This isn't anything new that he's doing."

Baseball can serve as a reprieve from the everyday challenges of life. However, the nature of the unrest was something most of the players and management had never experienced. It was also evident that more challenging times were still ahead. The situation simply was not going to die down after just one night. Darker days were on the horizon. Showalter was trying to make sense of the situation by trying to understand both sides. However, everyone, including city officials, remained stumped about what to do next and how to fix the situation.

"Obviously, my attention was elsewhere today with our family, but it's something that I'll probably have to get my arms around," Showalter said. "I'm not really there yet. But it's a challenging day for a lot of people, but probably a lot more than a baseball game. It's a game of baseball and those are life issues, so this kind of pales in comparison to what's going on in my life off the field and what's going on in our city. Just have to continue to have confidence that we'll get through it like we get through most things in Baltimore and hopefully learn from it."

After a stressful night, a quiet seemed to envelope the city the next day. Both the Orioles and Red Sox went about their usual routines. Still, there was no denying that the previous night's events had shaken everyone. The Red Sox players and coaches left the stadium together the previous night; there was no staggering out after a tough loss. When the first pitch was thrown shortly after 1:35 p.m., baseball once again gave the players and fans a reprieve from their troubles. The Orioles crushed the Red Sox 18–7 and there were no further related incidents reported in the city. Camden Yards drew 43,802 for that game, the last of the series, and Showalter made sure he thanked the fans for the support in such a tumultuous time.

He was once again impressed by the loyalty of Orioles Nation.

"I was curious to see how many people we would have today," Showalter said. "That was pretty impressive. I really thank them, too. They had something to do with that game today. There was a great feel in the ballpark, more than just baseball. To have that many people show up tells you how much they love the Orioles and how much confidence they have in this city. Pretty impressive. Doesn't go unnoticed."

On Monday, April 27, 2015, the tensions escalated again, and this time, at a much more alarming rate. There were more riots as looting and vandalism erupted on the western edge of the city. Students converged to confront police, who were hit with rocks and other objects. It was chaos as several fires were set in downtown Baltimore. The National Guard was eventually called to help contain the situation, which had residents frightened. The Orioles were forced to cancel their game with the White Sox that night. There was tension in the air as players watched the violence unfold on televisions in both clubhouses. While it was difficult to concentrate on baseball, the players were still ready to play a game until the decision was made for a postponement.

Once again, Showalter did not back down from the controversy and he addressed the issue in his pregame meeting with the media. He voiced sympathy for everyone that was affected by the unrest. Baseball was ready to take a backseat until order was restored. Major League Baseball Commissioner Rob Manfred was at the stadium for a previously planned visit and was forced to address the situation with the media.

"We feel like we made the decision that would provide us the greatest possible security in terms of protecting the fans, the players, the umpires, everybody involved in the game," Manfred said. "I don't know what more I can say about it at this point."

There was simply no way the teams could have played that evening. It would have compromised the safety of the fans, players, and all of the workers at Camden Yards. Showalter not only empathized with the city, but he also took some time to acknowledge what the players were feeling. They were caught in the middle of a situation they had no power to affect. Most of the players remained stoic in the face of this adversity. The White Sox were generally confused because they had no idea they would be traveling into such a hornet's nest. They faced being locked down at their hotel until further notice. Still, the players' inconvenience was overshadowed by the uncertainty facing Baltimore, which was in a full-blown crisis.

"There's so many things that go on that you get challenged with, obviously this is a different level," Showalter said. "There's not a lot of experience with it. So you try to take each moment as it comes and I know there were a lot of calls to some guys' families about making sure they knew what was going on from a safety standpoint. But guys are watching it. They are all aware of what's going on."

The problems continued as Baltimore was also forced to cancel the second game of the White Sox series because downtown was too dangerous. Baltimore Mayor Stephanie Rawlings-Blake instituted a curfew at 10:00 p.m. Everyone had to be off the streets and businesses were forced to close, which cost them, in aggregate, according to the *Baltimore Sun*, an estimated $9 million. Many store owners were trying to figure out what to do with their looted businesses. Some said they would be forced to close for good because they simply could not overcome the losses incurred from damage and expenses. Few people could recall such upheaval in the city.

The unrest was also creating havoc to the Orioles schedule. Because Chicago was not going to make any more appearances in Baltimore for the rest of the season, the games had to be made up on off-days and possibly with doubleheaders. Major League Baseball players have little time off during the season, so this created a challenge, especially for those who use those days to rest injuries or work with trainers. It's also inconvenient for the fans, who may not be able to attend the makeup games and lose money on the tickets. Still, Showalter was not about to complain about the inconvenience of it all, considering the circumstances.

"Everything in life, this too shall pass," he said. "Something's bad if you keep repeating it. We hope to take out of it a starting point for our city. The curfew put us in a challenge to play games at night."

As a result of the riots and the need to play games, the Orioles and Major League Baseball came to a drastic decision: Baltimore and Chicago would play the final game of the series at Camden Yards, but would not allow any fans. This was a safety measure and the police simply did not have the resources to allocate officers to a baseball game when another riot could break out at any time. It was believed to be the first Major League Baseball game played with no one in attendance except the media, scouts, and, of course, the players and team personnel. The teams were scheduled to make up the other two games with a double-header one month later. The Orioles players, however, could see the bigger picture. Adam Jones took a minute to speak directly to the Baltimore residents. Words from a professional athlete might resonate more than city officials in this particular case. Jones grew up in the city of San Diego and identified with how young people sometimes struggle. He said many kids just need "hugs" and love.

"People are hurting," Jones said. "As one of the older guys in the community, we owe it to the youth to continue to strengthen them, to educate them, to be by their sides. They don't need more antagonizing, they need a shoulder to cry on, and this city can be that for those kids," he continued.

The ballpark was very quiet, with almost an eerie feel to it, when the Orioles played the Chicago White Sox on April 29. Fans were not allowed in for safety reasons, due to rioting that had been happening in Baltimore for the few days before that.

It made for a surreal day at Camden Yards on April 29, 2015. The Orioles players actually seemed to add a little levity to the otherwise uncanny situation, throwing baseball into the empty stands at the end of an inning. Orioles catcher Caleb Joseph pretended to greet fans who were not there.

Baltimore also handled the situation better than Chicago did on the field, as Chris Davis hit a three-run homer onto Eutaw Street and the Orioles capitalized on a six-run first inning en route to an 8–2 victory. A small group of Orioles fans cheered for each hit and defensive play from outside the locked gates just past center field. They even enjoyed the seventh-inning stretch. Once the Orioles got into the game, it was simply a matter of playing baseball. Showalter once again had his players ready for the difficult situation. In the end, though, it was a day no one would ever forget, or want to experience again.

The sunshine was beautiful but the riots were still simmering several blocks away so the historic decision was made to lock out fans on April 29. Looking back, the move proved to be a smart one. It gave police and security that much less to worry about.

"Coming up the runway and walking out, it's kind of like batting practice," Showalter told a group of media after the game. "When we hit, nobody's here yet. You realize that you're a few minutes away from playing a major league baseball game that's going to count. You tried to stay focused on the competition, us trying to get where we want to be at the end of the season. But I also talked to them about the people who are going to be sitting around our city watching this game [on TV]. How many things have [been] normal here in the last few days in our society?"

The White Sox appeared to struggle to adjust to the surrealness of the day. Some players admitted that the game was one of the toughest they ever had to play. For one, it was not easy being stuck in a hotel for two days while riots raged a few blocks away. Players had to tell family members to stay away. By the time the game ended, the White Sox were ready to head to Minnesota to begin the next series and return to a normal routine.

The ballpark looked empty from every angle the day it was closed to the public and the Orioles and White Sox played ball.

"It was just a surreal environment," White Sox manager Robin Ventura said after the game. "I really don't think we want to play in another one like this. I don't think they do either."

But the inconvenience didn't end there for the Orioles.

Because of further instability in the city and ongoing protests, compounded with the challenge of the curfew, the Orioles' three-game series with the Rays was moved from Baltimore to Tampa Bay. What made the situation even more odd was that the Orioles were considered the "home" team down in Tampa. The series was not going to be made up in Baltimore at all. Instead, the Oriole bird mascot traveled with the team, Tampa Bay offered Baltimore food staples such as crab cakes and Bergers cookies, and John Denver's "Thank God I'm A Country Boy" was played during the seventh inning stretch.

Nonetheless, it was another challenge that the players had to overcome. While it was technically a "home" game on the schedule—the first of three in Tampa Bay—Tropicana Field was no Camden Yards, despite the proliferation of Orioles fans in attendance. Showalter was diplomatic about the pomp and circumstance following a 2–0 loss in the series opener. He was taking everything in stride and his players were following his example.

"Not really," said Showalter, when asked if the change in venue had led to the loss. "It'd be a very convenient excuse. It might seem strange, but once the game starts they're doing something they've done their whole lives. We pitched real well. They just pitched a little better."

From there, though, Showalter got the team back on track after the early doldrums. Baltimore's bats came alive and the Orioles took the next two games of the series against the Rays. The starting pitching that struggled over the first couple of weeks of the season became a strength.

There was that familiar energy in the clubhouse. After all, the Orioles were the defending American League East champions and had every intention to successfully defend that crown.

More importantly, Baltimore managed to overcome a myriad of injuries to shortstop J. J. Hardy and catcher Matt Wieters to get out of the first month of the season in solid shape. The series-clinching win against Tampa Bay on May 4 put the Orioles one game over .500 and in second place behind the Yankees. Despite the challenges, the players were not about to feel sorry for themselves. They were as stoic as their manager, who never once appeared concerned. Instead, he instilled more confidence in his players by consistently lauding and defending them in public.

"People have been through worse, man," Adam Jones said. "We're athletes. There's more people in Baltimore that are facing tougher hardships than we're facing. We get to play baseball for a living. You've got to look at the people that actually have to face some hardships. Those are the people back in Baltimore right now."

Chapter Ten
THE RETURN

The Orioles played their first game at Camden Yards in over two weeks on May 11 against American League East rival Toronto. The Orioles wore "Baltimore" emblazoned across the front of their home jerseys for the first time as a sign of solidarity with their beleaguered city.

The new look impressed the manager.

"I liked it. Really like the part that says 'Baltimore,'" Showalter said. "Good looking. I wasn't sure if they made one for me. A guy my age, you have to make sure things fit. How did I look?"

Showalter seems to always make the effort to express the pride he feels about being part of the Baltimore community. On October 19, 2014, the Baltimore Ravens saluted the Orioles for their playoff run with a video tribute. Showalter then was introduced on the field to a loud, standing ovation. He appeared to tear up at the reception. The Baltimore community responded to his loyalty and success with the team.

So, when the Orioles returned home on that warm May day, Showalter chose not to wear his usual pullover. Instead, he chose to wear the traditional jersey with "Baltimore" across the front. Again, it was a subtle gesture that went over huge with the local community.

"I'm very proud of Baltimore. I thought it was . . . Everybody wore it. And it fit," he joked.

There was a palpable excitement surrounding the game as the city continued to heal. Some fans even started a grassroots campaign on social media calling the game "Re-Opening Day." Showalter lauded the city for its commitment and loyalty to the team. On the field, Davis, Jones, and Machado homered and Ubaldo Jimenez had another dominant outing as the Orioles won 5–2. The win was even more special because it came against the Blue Jays, who were becoming the team's most bitter rival for the 2015 season.

Showalter cited one particular moment that resonated with him during the game, when Toronto first baseman Edwin Encarnacion lost the grip to his bat and it flew into the stands.

"Remember when Encarnacion threw the bat down the left field line, and our fans handed the bat back to him," Showalter said. "That touched my heart. I don't know why. That doesn't happen many places."

On the field, Showalter had to make several adjustments as injuries mounted, especially with the middle of the infield. Gold Glove shortstop J. J. Hardy missed the first five weeks of the season with an injured left shoulder. Second baseman Jonathan Schoop got knocked out of the lineup with a partially torn right knee ligament (plus the sprain of another) and didn't return until July 5. Utility infielder Ryan Flaherty, who Showalter praised for his versatility and effort, went back on the disabled list, just four days after his return, when he reinjured his right groin.

"We've got a very unconventional roster with the three outfielders and a catcher on the bench," Showalter said. "It really challenges the versatility of our players."

Flaherty was forced to go on the DL and Baltimore promoted infielder Rey Navarro from Triple-A Norfolk to take his spot. Steve Pearce was also a valuable commodity to Showalter because of his ability to play any position. Showalter had so much confidence in Pearce that he played the versatile infielder at second base even though he had never played there previously.

Pearce was another player who found a new lease on his career while playing for the Orioles. Showalter provided several guys an opportunity to play, and it was their responsibility to make the most of that chance. Pearce was originally picked up by the Orioles from the Yankees for cash considerations on June 2, 2012. Just over a month later, the Orioles designated him for assignment.

After a stint in Houston and a return to the Yankees that season, Pearce was once again picked up in September by the Orioles, who claimed him off waivers. The following season, Pearce made 44 appearances and hit .261 with four homers and 13 RBIs as a utility player. That was enough to earn him another one-year deal with the Orioles in 2014, but he was eventually released on April 27 because of a roster crunch. Pearce, however, was confident he could earn playing time with the team because Showalter was willing to give him an opportunity. So instead of moving to another team, Pearce re-signed with the Orioles just two days after being released.

From there, he became one of the team's most productive players and was vital to the Orioles' playoff run that season. He wound up setting career highs for almost every offensive category. Over 102 games (338 at bats), he hit .293 with 21 home runs and 49 RBIs. He also got 26 doubles and scored 51 runs. He continued to be a go-to guy for Showalter in 2015, playing different spots due to early-season injuries.

Showalter is a master of handling a roster. Every Major League Baseball team is beset with injuries throughout the course of a season, and the good teams know how to over-come those challenges. The Orioles pitching staff was hit with a spate of injuries in mid-May 2015. Bud Norris came down with bronchitis and Chris Tillman was dealing with a lower back strain. With the bats struggling for parts of the month, Showalter had to make some adjustments. To compound the problem, the Orioles had lost the first two games to the deep and talented Angels, and were looking to avoid a debilitating sweep.

What did Showalter do under the pressure? He handed the ball to a rookie who had never ever appeared in a Major League Baseball game.

"Mike Wright's going to start," Showalter said following a 6–1 loss to Los Angeles. "I let them know. He was aware of the possibility. There were people who were options. He's just ready to go. Really, you don't want to have him sit any longer, either. Mac helps us in long relief if we need it. We had one option at Triple-A, really, the way the schedule fell and who was there. Try to see how it goes tomorrow and looking forward to watching him pitch. He's another one of those guys we think highly of. He's physically ready to go and hopefully he'll be able to present himself well against a good club. That's the team with the best record in the American League last year that we're facing. They're a good club. Very fundamentally sound."

Once again, the manager looked smart with the decision, as Wright shined in his debut, throwing 7 1/3 scoreless innings with six strikeouts and no walks.

After the game, Showalter praised the young pitcher's performance. Once again, the Orioles' minor league depth that took so long to build was paying dividends. Baltimore stocked its affiliates with young, capable arms and some of them were thriving in the system. When these young players got an opportunity with the big league club, Showalter was quick to publicly praise them.

"His presentation was real confident," Showalter said about Wright. "He's done some things the way it used to be done, where you make every stop [in the minors]. And you do things at a level [and] you're not wondering if you had done real well at the level you left. That's the blueprint of coming through [to the majors]."

The month of May also signified the return of Nelson Cruz, the former Oriole who signed with Seattle as a free agent during the off-season. While playing for the Rangers in 2013, Cruz received a 50-game suspension for violating the league's Basic Agreement and its Joint Drug Prevention and Treatment program. Cruz did not appeal the suspension, which began immediately. Following the season, Cruz declined a $14 million qualifying offer from the Rangers to become a free agent but didn't find many potential suitors.

The Orioles responded with a one-year, $8 million offer that he accepted. He took full advantage of the opportunity and resurrected his career with a monster season. Cruz led the majors with 40 home runs and also played a vital role in helping the team win the American League East. He also had a team-leading 108 RBIs, in addition to batting .271. The Baltimore media named Cruz as the "Most Valuable Oriole." Cruz is most remembered for playing a huge role in the Orioles' American League East championship last season, and the fans showed their appreciation.

However, Baltimore and Cruz could not agree to terms to extend their relationship for a few more seasons. As a result, Cruz took advantage of his sensational season and signed a four-year, $57 million deal with the Mariners.

In his return to Camden Yards, Cruz was hoping to get some "love" from the Orioles fans and that's exactly what he received. The fans cheered when he was first introduced and then provided more support each time he came to the plate. The Baltimore fans even cheered when he crushed his league-leading sixteenth homer in the fourth inning off Miguel Gonzalez. Cruz was grateful for the response and lauded his time with the Orioles. He took time the entire series to reflect on his stellar season.

"It was a blast," Cruz said about returning to Baltimore."We accomplished something special as a team. It was a great time. Great teammates."

Showalter remained diplomatic about the decision to not keep Cruz, and was careful not to criticize his bosses for being too frugal.

"He handled himself with a lot of class here," Showalter said. "He had some big hits for us. He enjoys winning."

By the end of a tough stretch in the early part of the 2015 season, Showalter found his leadership challenged again. This time, left-handed reliever Brian Matusz was ejected from a May 23 game against the Marlins for having a banned substance on his right arm. Matusz was also suspended eight games by Major League Baseball. Because the Orioles could not replace him, Showalter was left with a short bench. Instead of publicly calling out Matusz for his indiscretion, Showalter once again defended his player. He also voiced some support for fellow reliever T. J. McFarland, who was forced into action when Matusz was ejected and eventually took the loss.

"It's one of those things that publicly you're always supportive of your players," Showalter said. "Privately, you're always trying to make people aware of their actions. I'm sure T. J. McFarland has some ideas about it. A lot of people are affected by things."

The foreign substance used by Matusz was widely believed to have been sunscreen and rosin—two items believed to be essential to any pitcher, but not necessarily within the rules of the game. Showalter, who has long lauded the Japanese version of a baseball, which is easier to grip because it's slightly smaller, commented on the bigger issue of pitchers being able to adequately grip the ball.

"We've all got a personal opinion about the crux of where it all comes from, especially baseball people," he said. "Hopefully, it's something we'll attack finally and get right. I think it's something that's really drawing attention to the challenge pitchers have . . . Hitters can grip the bat, but pitchers can't (use the same thing). Gloves. Catching gear. There are so many things. Why does a guy wear glasses as an umpire?"

Chapter Eleven

LARGER THAN LIFE

Showalter's charisma extends beyond the baseball diamond. He has appeared on David Letterman, was featured in an episode of *Seinfeld*, and was a commentator for ESPN. The general public relates to his humble personality, despite his success as a manager and analyst. Showalter's approachability and southern twang has appealed to a mass audience.

Showalter appeared on the *David Letterman Show* on May 3, 1992, when he was managing the New York Yankees, with his hitting coach Frank Howard. The goal was to teach Letterman about some of the scoop from inside the dugout, such as chatter and heckling from the dugout, the use of spitting tobacco, and getting hit by a pitch. These are typical goings on that Showalter witnessed over the years as both a player and manager.

The sketch took place at the Yankees' spring training facility in Fort Lauderdale, Florida. Showalter proved to be a natural in front of the camera.

When Letterman announced his retirement from CBS is 2015, Showalter reminisced about the time he appeared on the show.

"I remember the first time they called we were in Fort Lauderdale in spring training and they wanted to know if I would call in to the *Letterman* show," Showalter said. "I'm going, 'Wow. Call in?' So I did after the workout . . . the first question was, 'Buck, when you are on the back fields and you're doing drills and stuff, what are you really working on, what are you doing?' I went, 'We're kind of working on fundamentals.' And I heard the audience laugh and I heard 'ding, ding, ding.' So I'm putting two and two together that he's trying to see how many baseball cliches he can get me to say in like two minutes. I found out later there was like this big board (with words). And so the next question he asked me was, 'Buck, do you start thinking about all of spring training or three games in advance or how do you take each game?' And I knew it. So I said, 'David, I guess you want me to say I take them one game at a time.' And I heard 'ding, ding, ding' again and he cut off the interview, right there."

Showalter is not someone who puts on airs. What you see, is what you get. That is one of the reasons he is so comfortable in front of the camera.

That was also apparent on the *Seinfeld* episode that appeared September 22, 1994, called "The Chaperone." One of the subplots of the episode is when the character George Costanza, who is the assistant to the travelling secretary for the Yankees, decides to replace New York's polyester uniforms with cotton ones. Showalter, then the Yankees manager, guest stars as himself and has to deal with Costanza and his absurd idea.

Costanza convinces Showalter that cotton uniforms would be more comfortable for the players. Of course, this turns out to be an unwise decision, since the cotton shrinks during a rainy game, forcing the Yankees "to run like penguins."

Following his tenure with the Diamondbacks, which ended after the 2000 season, Showalter found his way back to television. Instead of comedy and fiction, he joined ESPN as

Orioles manager Buck Showalter is very good at dealing with the media.

an analyst and almost immediately thrived in the position. His knowledge of the game captivated viewers and also brought a new dimension to the broadcast. Showalter would have two stints with the network. He first left ESPN to take a job with the Rangers in 2003, but then returned to ESPN after the 2006 season. Both times it was a seamless transition from the dugout to the studio. Showalter had an instant, easy rapport with his fellow broadcasters and that translated to successful chemistry that resonated with audiences.

The job at ESPN also provided him an opportunity to take a broader, more objective look at Major League Baseball and see the game from a different perspective. His knowledge and love of the game was an appealing attribute for the network. His ability to unveil the subtle nuances of the game and his overall management style caught the eye of the upper management of the Baltimore Orioles, who were struggling with a decade of losing and indifference from the fans. With Showalter, the Orioles were confident they had finally found a savior to lead the team back to its former prominence. Baltimore had won the World Series in 1966, 1970, and 1993 and were one of Major League Baseball's most storied franchises.

After making the playoffs in back-to-back years in 1996 and 1997, the Orioles had fallen on hard times. The organization gutted the roster, casting aside several key players and fan favorites. Rumors of discord plagued the front office. This ultimately led to fourteen consecutive losing seasons with little hope in sight. Everything changed when Showalter took the job on July 29, 2010, following the departure of Juan Samuel. Showalter was quick to credit his experience at ESPN for the opportunity.

"My job with ESPN allowed me to follow this organization closely over the last several years, and although the current record may seem to indicate otherwise, I see enormous potential with this club," Showalter said. "I look forward to the challenge of competing in the American League East. Baltimore is a tremendous baseball town with passion and pride in its club, and my family and I look forward to making it our new home."

Chapter Twelve

THE GNOME

Showalter was not exactly thrilled when the Orioles' promotions department sponsored "Buck Showalter Garden Gnome Day" on June 27, 2015. It initially appeared the baseball gods agreed with his reservations because the scheduled game that day against the Indians was postponed due to the presence of violent storms in the area most of the day. "I haven't seen it," said Showalter when asked about the gnome. "I will not see it. I asked them not to do it, and they did it anyway. I said, 'Why did you ask me if you're going to do it anyway?'"

Despite the manager's reservations, there would be no stopping the garden gnome. The Orioles simply rescheduled the promotion for the night cap the following day as part of a split doubleheader. At that point, Showalter was too busy organizing his pitching staff to be worried about some ceramic, 10-inch gnome that apparently looked nothing like him. Fans, however, were charged with excitement. Anticipation for the giveaway had reached a fever pitch among the local fan base. The Orioles were only giving out 25,000 statues, so there was inevitably going to be heated competition to snag one.

The day could not have started better for the Orioles, who won the first game of the doubleheader against Cleveland, 4–0, before a sellout crowd. Ubaldo Jimenez continued his resurgence and threw eight innings of four-hit ball to pick up his fourth straight win.

But there was more baseball to play that day and boxes of garden gnomes to give away.

After the first game ended, the excitement was palpable. Hundreds of fans were already lined up outside Camden Yards anxiously awaiting for the gates to open. When stadium staff finally unlocked the stadium at 5:25 p.m. EST, there was a cheer among the fans who were like children at Christmas eagerly awaiting to tear open presents.

The fun, however, did not stop there. The Orioles players made sure the garden gnome had a spot on the railing at the top of the dugout through parts of the game. But they made sure to keep the caricature out of their manager's sight line. Showalter would probably not have been amused. Hell hath no fury like a baseball manager scorned.

On the field, the Orioles were dominant again. Chris Davis, Travis Snider, and Chris Parmelee hit home runs and the Orioles completed the sweep with an 8–0 victory, moving Baltimore into a virtual tie with Tampa Bay for first place in the American League East for the first time since April 19. Chris Tillman, who had anchored the Orioles rotation for the past two seasons but had some struggles in 2015, won for the fourth time in his past five starts. He threw seven innings of four-hit ball with six strikeouts and he did not allow a walk.

Some theorists were adamant the garden gnome played a role in the good fortune.

Following the game. the reporters put the garden gnome on the desk where Showalter conducts his postgame news conference. The microphone was even lowered so it appeared the gnome was speaking to the media. When Showalter entered, he did not even crack a smile. But in the end, Showalter seemed to take it in stride and finally was at peace with the gnome.

"All kidding aside, it is an honor," Showalter said. "I get it, if that's the right word. I'll be glad when the sun comes up tomorrow and we move on to another promotion."

It was difficult to argue over the gnome's popularity. Some entrepreneurial fans were ambitious enough to put the gnome on eBay, where they were fetching almost $90 apiece just hours after the game. Showalter was astonished by this news the following day. It remains to be seen if he would ever agree to a similar promotion. Nonetheless, he was humbled by the attention.

"You know what, it's like autographs," he said. "When you've gotta worry is when they quit asking."

Promotions centering around Showalter didn't end at the garden gnome. The Orioles have also given away several T-shirts as promotions that referenced Showalter. Throughout his time with the Orioles, Showalter developed a catch-phrase, "I like our guys," that he used repeatedly in his pre-game and postgame meetings with reporters. It became so popular with the fans and organization, the Orioles had an "I like our guys" promotional T-shirt giveaway on May 1, 2014, against the Pirates. To give the phrase even more gravitas, the names of all of the Orioles players that made the 40-man roster were on the back of the shirt within an angry-looking cartoon Oriole Bird. After the Orioles swept a doubleheader against the Pirates that day, Showalter offered more confirmation in his postgame news conference.

"I told you I like our guys," he said, breaking up the room.

Chapter Thirteen
THE JONES FACTOR

Center fielder Adam Jones arrived in Baltimore two years prior to Showalter. At the time they acquired Jones in 2008, the Orioles were well out of contention and willing to trade veteran players for talented younger ones to build for the future. That deal wound up laying the foundation for success in the coming years, with players like Jones and pitcher Chris Tillman playing vital roles for the club.

Jones joined the Orioles organization on February 8, 2008, in a trade with Seattle. Baltimore received Jones and Tillman, along with reliever George Sherrill and minor league pitchers Kam Mickolio and Tony Butler in exchange for the mercurial left-handed starting pitcher Erik Bedard.

Andy MacPhail, the Orioles president of baseball operations at the time, was prophetic in his analysis of the trade at the time.

"We traded one of the game's best young left-handed pitchers, but in exchange we think we improved the long-term outlook for the Baltimore Orioles," MacPhail said. "There aren't too many five-for-one trades anymore. We are delighted to have all five in the system."

Jones was immediately given the opportunity to make an impact with the Orioles. He played in 132 games in the 2008 season with the club and batted .270 with nine home runs and 57 RBIs. He showed flashes of being one of the five-tool players Baltimore had long-coveted and was 11th in the American League with seven triples. He endeared himself to Orioles fans by hitting a grand slam against the Yankees on July 28. Furthermore, he covered a lot of ground in center field.

The Orioles, however, finished 68–93 and in last place in the American League East. Baltimore also finished 28.5 games behind first-place Tampa Bay, which frustrated fans even further.

In Jones's second year, the Orioles were even worse, finishing the season with a 64–98 record, once again good for last place. This added more angst in Orioles Nation because it was the fifth straight year the team finished with fewer wins than the prior season. The Yankees won the division as Baltimore finished an astounding 39 games behind them. Only the Washington Nationals and Pittsburgh Pirates had worse records than Baltimore. Manager Dave Trembley was feeling the heat.

In his second year with the team, Jones was one of the few bright spots that season. He appeared in 119 games, batting .277 with 19 homers and 70 RBIs, despite being hampered by an ankle injury during the second half of the season. Jones was fifth among major league outfielders with five assists and won the Gold Glove. He also represented the Orioles in the All-Star Game and knocked in the game-winning run on a sacrifice fly. It was one of the few moments Orioles fans had a chance to cheer that entire season.

Jones did not visibly show any negative effects from the losing. Other players showed some frustration and voiced concern, but Jones simply came to work and did his job. He served as a prime example of the strategy at that time—to

Adam Jones has emerged as a true leader in the Baltimore clubhouse and has a good relationship with manager Buck Showalter.

build a solid team with young players from their farm system and other organizations.

With a farm system finally full of potential and some young players ready to take over a spot in the everyday lineup and rotation, there was actually optimism heading into the 2010 season. It was supposed to be the year Baltimore finally turned the corner after more than a decade of losing. The Orioles did in fact begin to make their way in the right direction, but it was not the path most expected.

The 2010 season brought a series dramatic change to the Baltimore Orioles. Dave Trembley was fired from the team June 4. He had been at the helm less than three years and compiled a 187–283 record. Few people were surprised at the move. Baltimore then decided to hire Juan Samuel for the position and it was an uphill fight from the very beginning with the team mired in last place in the AL East. Despite a couple of four-game winning streaks, the team continued to struggle. Samuel's tenure came to an end on August 1 following a

5–4 loss to Kansas City. The Orioles had already announced Showalter's hiring on July 29 so Samuel knew he was a lame duck. He finished 17–34 in his short tenure. Showalter agreed to take over the club August 2 and Samuel decided to leave the club entirely to pursue other opportunities.

Through all of this upheaval, Jones remained diplomatic and was always available to offer a comment about the team's struggles. He had already shown his support for the new manager by attending Showalter's press conference with several other Orioles employees.

As Jones sat in the back of the press conference, Showalter confidently answered questions, including one that dealt with his perceived micromanaging style.

"I try to be true to my own skin," Showalter said. "I am who I am. I don't spend a lot of time over-analyzing it. I know what's worked for me with the organizations I've been with in the past."

Nonetheless, there was palpable excitement when Showalter took over. He immediately recognized how important Jones was to the team. Jones had solidified his position in center field and that was one game-day decision Showalter would never have to worry about.

In the 2010 season, Jones posted a .284 batting average with 19 homers, 69 RBIs, and 7 stolen bases. He also continued to shine defensively, and led all major league center fielders with 12 assists. Showalter began to refer to him as "A. J." in his sessions with the media, and everyone could see how their relationship as manager and player was blossoming.

The expectations for the 2011 season were soaring for both Jones and the entire Orioles organization, especially after the strong finish in 2010. By the time the 2011 season began, Jones was ostensibly the face of the franchise. He met those high hopes by having the best season of his young career, batting .280 with a then-career-high 25 home runs and 83 RBIs, as well as once again a stellar performance in the outfield. He avoided major injuries, produced in the middle of the lineup, and had a solid rapport with the fans.

But the year also brought uncertainty to the club, which as a whole fell mostly flat. Despite several impressive winning streaks, the Orioles finished the season at 69–93, 28 games behind the first-place New York Yankees. Orioles President of Baseball Operations Andy MacPhail's contract expired after the season and he voluntarily stepped down. There was speculation that Showalter would move from the dugout and into the front office. Ultimately, he decided to stay as the manager and the Orioles hired Dan Duquette to lead the front office as executive vice president, baseball operations. It was a seemingly bold move, as Duquette had been out of the game for nine years after building the Red Sox into a World Series contender.

The Orioles had a busy offseason and signed a couple of lesser-known international pitchers—Wei-Yin Chen and

Wei-Yin Chen and Orioles manager Buck Showalter hug after a game. Chen's consistency as a starter was one of the team's bright points in 2015.

Miguel Gonzalez—who wound up being a fixture in their rotation for years to come.

The lineup in 2012 revolved around Jones, who started strong and never cooled down. Over the first two months of the season, Jones hit .310 with 14 homers and 31 RBIs. The San Diego native also solidified his commitment to the Orioles organization by signing a six-year, $85.5 million contract extension, making him the highest paid center fielder in all of Major League Baseball. Jones also endeared himself to the local community.

"I fit here in this city. I fit here on this team. I fit in Camden Yards. I don't see myself wearing another white uniform that doesn't have 'Orioles' across the chest," Jones said at his press conference to announce the contract. "I'm not from Baltimore. This is now my town."

The deal also showed the Orioles were finally committed to winning after enduring fourteen consecutive losing seasons that alienated much of the fan base. With Jones as a fixture in the lineup and expressing optimism about the future, the City of Baltimore was getting back on the Orioles bandwagon. When Jones signed the contract, the Orioles were in first place in the American League East with a 29–18 record. Fans were starting to believe the giant was about to wake from its long slumber.

"We have to prove to the fans that we're for real," Jones said. "We're slowly doing it. This is a big step in that right direction. There's a bigger goal here, I believe, and that's winning games."

With the contract issue behind him, Jones thrived and was named to the 2012 All-Star team. He also hit a career-high 32 home runs and was named the Most Valuable Oriole for the second straight season.

As a team, the Orioles were also excelling. The good vibes started on May 6 when they beat the Red Sox 9–6 in 17 innings. Chris Davis, who started the game as the designated hitter, was forced to pitch the final two innings. He did not allow a run and picked up his first and only career victory. Jones hit the game-winning three-run homer in the 17th inning off Red Sox outfielder and former Oriole Darnell McDonald.

"Just when you think you've seen it all, some days you come out here and just assume the position. That was fun," Showalter said after the game. "It was a long day, but you like to get something good out of it."

The victory had fans cheering back home. The Orioles had not only beaten the Red Sox in a heart-breaking fashion just as they had at the end of 2011, but they sent the Red Sox into last place. The Yankees were mired in the fourth spot. While it was still early in the season, it was the first time Boston and New York were that far down in the division.

As the season progressed, outsiders were waiting for the Orioles' inevitable collapse. But it never happened. Baltimore continued to roll and on September 13, the team finally clinched its first non-losing season in fourteen years with a 3–2 victory over the Rays in 14 innings. Manny Machado got the game-winning hit with a bloop single. Despite the milestone, Showalter and the rest of the team knew there was more work to be done.

"There's a bigger goal in mind," Showalter said. "That wasn't the goal from Day One this spring. Really, Day One of the offseason. It's watching other teams for years and saying, 'We want to do what they're doing.' We'd like to get a chair at the dance, you know?"

The Orioles did not slow down and finished the regular season with a 93–69 record, two games behind the Yankees, who recovered from their early-season doldrums. That was good enough for Baltimore to clinch one of two wild card playoff spots in the American League. This set them up for a matchup with the powerful Rangers and their dominant ace Yu Darvish in Arlington, Texas.

While few people outside the organization gave the Orioles much of a chance, Baltimore dominated the entire game and rolled to a 5–1 victory. Jones batted fourth and knocked in what proved to be the winning run in the sixth inning with a sacrifice fly. The Orioles won their first playoff game in fifteen years.

"With our team, it's just a bunch of guys that raised the bar and wouldnt give in and still haven't," Showalter said after the game. "Now they get a chance to win to roll the dice, and there's a lot of good card players in there."

The victory meant a showdown with Showalter's former team, the New York Yankees, in the best-of-five division series. It was a David vs. Goliath showdown when taking into account each of the team's recent history. The Orioles pushed the Yankees before falling in five games. The final game, a 3–1 Baltimore loss, had some controversy as what appeared to be a pivotal home run by Orioles outfielder Nate McLouth was called foul by the umpires. However, the loss didn't diminish what the Orioles accomplished that season.

"It's been about as much fun as I have had in the big leagues watching how they play the game every day, the standard they held themselves to and the way they raised the bar in Baltimore with each other," Showalter said.

Jones's success could mirror how well the Orioles were doing as a team. He continued to represent the organization well and Showalter was quick to point out the center fielder's importance to the clubhouse. For his continued development as a player, Jones was named to the United States squad for the 2013 World Baseball Classic. One of the highlights of that tournament was against Canada, when Jones had three RBIs to help the US advance to second round. Jones was honored to be part of the team and be around some of the game's top players.

"I think it's going to be an experience of a lifetime," Jones told MLB.com. "This is an All-Star contest. It's the Olympics, basically. Team USA is trying to get the best players they can. I know the Japanese take tremendous pride in whooping everybody's butt the first two, so, USA, let's go."

While trying to help the US win, Jones made sure playing in the tournament would not affect his performance with the Orioles over the course of a 162-game Major League Baseball season. Jones was a vital cog to the Orioles' machine and an injury to him could derail the season. Jones was not afraid to address that issue with the media.

"I want them not to be worried about me," Jones said. "That's why I want to prepare myself the best, that's why I want to come in shape," Jones said. "The first couple days [this spring] is going to be work, work, work, because I'm going to have to be able to get myself ready to play center field. These [Classic] games mean a lot. Spring Training doesn't mean much, these games mean a lot. You got the whole country behind you."

That tournament set the tone for another dominant season. Jones batted .285 with a career-high 33 home runs. He also knocked in a career-best 108 runs. However, he did draw some criticism for not showing great discipline at the plate, registering just a .318 on-base percentage with only 25 walks. Still, Jones had developed into the type of player who could single-handedly take over a game. Showalter continuously praised him after games—whether the team won or lost. The two had developed a solid relationship.

The Orioles were trying to ride the success of the prior season's playoff run. The teams in the American League East, however, reloaded and in 2013 it was the most dominant division in all of baseball. Showalter managed to keep the team from taking a step back and going back to a losing season. Prior to the season, both Showalter and Duquette showed their commitment to the organization by signing contract extensions that ran through the 2018 season. Baltimore is the type of city that embraces loyalty. This meant the contract extensions made Showalter and Duquette local royalty.

The Orioles' ownership rarely addresses the media, but they took the opportunity at a press conference to laud the news.

"These are two highly accomplished, experienced baseball veterans who, in short order, have brought winning baseball back to Baltimore. They have done a fantastic job," said Louis Angelos, the son of owner Peter Angelos. "It sort of felt right for everybody."

With the immediate future set, Baltimore finished the year at a respectable 85–77, twelve games behind the first-place Red Sox in a division saturated with talent. The days of being out of the playoff chase by the All-Star break appeared to be over.

Jones's charisma led to him being asked to join the MLB Network as an analyst for the playoffs. Jones accepted and was every bit as comfortable as his manager in front of the camera.

Yet Jones wasn't the only Orioles player to shine in 2013. Despite the fourth-place finish, fans flocked to Camden Yards to watch Chris Davis, who enjoyed a break-out season with a league-leading 53 home runs. There was palpable excitement as he chased Brady Anderson, who held the franchise's previous single-season high with 50 in 1996. Davis also led the league with 138 RBIs and set another franchise record with 96 extra base hit.

Showalter's dedication to fundamentals and getting back to the "Oriole Way" also began to become a moniker of the franchise. Baltimore had three players—Jones, J. J. Hardy, and Manny Machado—take home Gold Gloves Awards following the season. Baltimore was also becoming more popular nationally with fans as five players—Jones, Davis, Hardy, Machado, and Chris Tillman—were named All-Stars that season. Showalter even garnered the lone third-place vote for the 2013 Manager of the Year.

So, despite some disappointment following a fourth-place finish, optimism abounded and the players and fans were looking forward to making another playoff run in 2013. The front office had finally found a balance between the major league roster and having depth and development in the minors. The results were finally showing and it was difficult to go anywhere in the Baltimore area without seeing someone wearing an Orioles hat or T-shirt.

The Orioles were aggressive heading into the 2014 season. They signed right-hander Ubaldo Jimenez to the biggest free agent contract in franchise history. Duquette also took a gamble and signed outfielder/designated hitter Nelson Cruz, who was coming off a suspension for using performance enhancing drugs.

Jones did not slow down and was named to the All-Star Game once again. Baltimore, however, finished the first month of the season in last place and then went on an impressive run to take over first place at the midseason break. Cruz and catcher Matt Wieters joined Jones on the American League All-Star team.

The Orioles continued to roll when play resumed in July. However, it appeared their playoff hopes took a hit when Machado went down with what ended up being a season-ending knee injury on August 11. Davis took over third base duties and Baltimore maintained its lead in the AL East.

By this time, anticipation was growing around the city for another playoff appearance. The long-suffering Orioles fans were on the verge of their second season of postseason baseball in three years. As Baltimore stayed more than eight games ahead of the second-place Yankees, the team was hit with yet another huge blow. Davis, who led the league in home runs the previous season, was suspended 25 games after a drug test revealed he had used an amphetamine without proper permission. This meant he would not be available for the rest of the regular season and the playoffs. The team, however, was resilient and were resigned to move on without him.

Publicly, the Orioles rallied around Davis for the crucial mistake. Jones took the lead for the players in addressing the situation to the media.

"It's unfortunate," Jones said. "He made a mistake. I'm sure he's regretting it. Us as a team, we stick by him and we still have faith in him. If and when he is able to come back, we'll assess that and see how it works. We support him. Bad move, bad decision, but we support him."

Baltimore proved to be just fine without Davis, as the Orioles clinched the American League East September 16 with an 8–2 victory over Toronto at Camden Yards. It was the Orioles' first division title since 1997 and it set off a wild celebration around the city. They were the second seed in the American League playoffs behind the Angels. The Orioles finished the season 96–66, 12 games ahead of the second-place Yankees. Baltimore's powerful lineup slugged a league-leading 211 home runs.

Jones finished the season batting .281 with 29 homers and 96 RBIs. He was a force all season and would once again be able to showcase his skills in front of a national audience in the playoffs. It was an opportunity Jones embraced as the de facto leader of the Orioles clubhouse.

Baltimore faced the Detroit Tigers in the American League Division Series. The Tigers were favored by many because of the pitching staff, led by Justin Verlander, and a powerful lineup anchored by Miguel Cabrera. The Orioles, however, got off to a splendid start with a 12–3 victory in Game 1. The crowd at Camden Yards roared with every successful play by the home team and turned the stadium into a sea of orange by waving bright Orioles towels. Even the unshakeable Showalter took notice.

"If you don't get that, you're too cold for his game," Showalter said. "I wish I would have had a towel."

The Tigers appeared on their way to evening the series in Game 2 with a three-run lead in the eighth inning. But the Orioles responded again as Delmon Young sparked a four-run rally that inning with a pinch-hit double that drove in three runs. The Orioles held on for a 7–6 victory to take a 2–0 lead in the best-of-five series. Baltimore was clicking on all cylinders, but since the series was heading to Detroit, some felt there could be a change in fortunes.

The Orioles, however, were simply too tough and completed the three-game sweep with a 2–1 victory. Cruz led the way with a two-run homer and Bud Norris outdueled a tough David Price.

"This is fun to watch. Believe me, I'm happier than you can imagine," Showalter said. "But most of it comes from getting to see the players get what they've put into it."

Jones and the rest of the players were confident they could make a run all the way to the franchise's first World Series since 1983. The Orioles had come close in 1996 and 1997 with two of their best teams, advancing to the American League Championship series in each of those season. However, the Orioles fell to the Yankees in 1996 in a series that would go down in infamy in Baltimore, when in Game 1, twelve-year-old Jeffrey Maier reached over the right field fence to snag a fly ball by Derek Jeter. The umpire gave Jeter a home run rather than ruling fan interference. That set the tone, and ultimately Baltimore lost the series 4–1. The following year, the Orioles had another strong team that owned the American League East for the entire season. However, after beating Seattle and Randy Johnson in the Division Series, the Orioles were upset by the Indians 4–2.

Following that run, the franchise took a turn for the worse until Showalter arrived. The city had embraced this new group of players, who had overcome the loss of Machado and Davis to win a playoff series. The players believed they had the talent to make a run to the October Classic.

"We've got a lot to go and we're grinding," Jones said. "If we play as a team, we can do anything."

The Orioles, however, ran into a team that was even hotter than them—the Kansas City Royals. Baltimore simply could not get anything going offensively in the American League Championship Series. The Royals, on the other hand, seemed to have everything break their way. In Game 1, Alex Gordon and Mike Moustakas each homered in the 10th inning to give the Royals an 8–6 victory. Jones went 1-for-5 with a key RBI, but it was simply not enough to seal the deal.

The second game didn't go much better for the Orioles. This time, Alcides Escobar hit an RBI double in the ninth and Kansas City prevailed with a 6–4 victory. Jones managed his first postseason homer with a two-run shot in the third. Despite being down two games to none, Jones and the rest of the Orioles believed they could get back in the series. They just needed to win a game to swing the momentum.

"The series ain't over," Jones said. "If you guys [are] thinking it's over, why are we going to show up on Monday?"

But things did not get better for the Orioles in Game 3. The bats struggled again and a sacrifice fly by Billy Butler in the sixth wound up being the difference in the Royals' 2–1 victory. After another stellar season, Baltimore was now in danger of being swept in four games. Jones again was the main voice in the Orioles' clubhouse and warned reporters not assume the series was over.

"It's been done before, so that gives you a chance," Jones said. "We've won four games before. Obviously, not in this situation. But we've won four games, four games, four games. So start tomorrow, start in the first inning and get some runs on the board."

The final indignity came October 16 in Game 4. The Royals scored twice in the first inning and their pitching did the rest in another 2–1 victory. Kansas City was headed back to the World Series for the first time since 1985—two years after the Orioles' last appearance. It was a disappointing finish for Baltimore, which had overcome so much adversity, including injuries to Machado and Wieters, along with the suspension of Davis, to come within four games of reaching the World Series.

Jones said his team should be proud of the season. Kansas City was simply better.

"They played really good baseball, and they deserve to go to the World Series," Jones said to reporters following the final game. "Not saying we don't. We just didn't win," Jones said. "This team that we have is unbelievable. It's been an unbelievable year. Obviously, we'd like to continue, but it didn't happen. To get this far with this group of men has been an honor. Everyone in here has meant the world to myself and to each other and to each other's families."

Like any good leader, Showalter took accountability for the loss. A couple of different decisions here and there might have made a difference, especially since the games were so close throughout the series. Despite all of his accomplishments, Showalter still had not won an American League Championship Series. Still, he was lauded back in Baltimore for his ability to steer the team through some unsteady water.

"I keep thinking about something I or we could have done differently. That's what you think about," Showalter said. "But if you care, like our people care, it hurts."

There was nothing left to do except look ahead to 2015. The Orioles had come a long way from fourteen straight losing seasons. Showalter had changed the entire culture of the franchise. The team had a solid group of players on its twenty-five-man roster and the minor league affiliates have depth and talent. There was little doubt among the players they could get back to the postseason if the front office could keep the core of the roster intact. However, there were several tough decisions facing Duquette and Showalter heading into the offseason. The most pressing was what to do with Cruz, who hit a league-leading 40 home runs and a career-high 108 RBI, single-handedly carrying the team throughout parts of the season. Baltimore had signed Cruz to a one-year deal and he was likely to command a high-asking price on the open market as a free agent.

Other key performers for the Orioles had another year left on their contracts. Wieters, Davis, and utility player Steve Pearce were locked up for 2015. Starting pitchers Wei-Yin Chen and Bud Norris, along with relievers Darren O'Day and Tommy Hunter, also had another year on their contracts before they could become free agents. So, once the disappointment of the playoff loss to Kansas City subsided, there was optimism among the front office and players about the 2015 season. Jones certainly was ready to get back to work.

"I think we can be even better," Jones said. "We've got this far and we've been down a couple guys for a couple months. But the guys that filled in are such special guys. It's going to be fun to come to spring training. We've been playing very good baseball for the past three years, and now we've just got to continue that and get over the hump."

Midway through the 2015 season, Jones hit a pair of homers against the Nationals, good for 180 as an Oriole. That was also good enough for eighth place all-time in Orioles' franchise history, allowing him to pass Hall of Famer Frank Robinson.

Chapter Fourteen

PROTECTING THE YARD

Oriole Park at Camden Yards was routinely sold out when the stadium opened to much fanfare on April 8, 1992. Camden Yards eventually became the standard for new baseball stadiums around the United States. The City of Baltimore was proud of the monument. Not only was it good for civic pride and tourism, but it also meant the Orioles would not be leaving town like the Baltimore Colts, who fled to Indianapolis in the middle of the night in March 1984. Orioles fans were always paranoid the team would run to nearby Washington for a sweeter deal. Hence, that scenario never materialized and the new, expensive stadium helped make sure of that.

The Orioles enjoyed early success in their new digs that replaced the aging Memorial Stadium. Baltimore did not have a losing record at Camden Yards until 2001. In the first six seasons, the franchise made the playoffs twice—in 1996 and 1997. The Orioles were also at the top of the league in attendance for much of the first decade Camden Yards opened. The tide, however, began to turn in 1998 and it would take years to rebound.

Following the playoff run in 1997, Orioles manager Davey Johnson, who brought the team back to prominence, decided to resign at the end of the season. Johnson and Orioles owner Peter Angelos butted heads throughout the manager's tenure. The relationship took an even worse turn in 1997 over mercurial second baseman Roberto Alomar, who decided to skip a team banquet and then blew off an exhibition game against the Orioles' Triple-A affiliate in Rochester. Alomar was fined $10,500 and was ordered to direct the money to a charity where Johnson's wife, Susan, worked. Angelos said that Johnson's decision to direct the fine to that charity was a conflict of interest. Johnson later agreed with that assessment, but the relationship was already beyond repair.

On November 5, Johnson faxed his resignation letter to Angelos, who accepted the decision. The letter arrived just hours after Johnson was named the American League Manager of the Year. Johnson went 186–138 over his two seasons in Baltimore.

"I'd been hoping that we could mend the fences and go on, but it became obvious that we couldn't," Johnson told Mark Maske of the *Washington Post*. "I'm not bitter. I'm thankful that he brought me there. I'm happy for that. We had two great years, I thought. I have a lot of friends in Baltimore. I love the team. I love the city. At least we put the Orioles on the right track."

From there, the Orioles went on a downward spiral that attracted national attention and it appeared they never would recover.

Starting in 1998, Baltimore endured fourteen straight losing seasons. The Orioles also went through six managers over that span, including Showalter, who was hired in 2010. It began with former pitching coach Ray Miller, who lasted for the 1998–99 season, going 157–167. The organization thought it solved the problem by replacing Miller with former Indians skipper Mike Hargrove. Hargrove, however, could not right the ship and he was fired in 2003 after three seasons when he compiled a 275–372 record. Next up was former Yankees coach Lee Mazzilli, who never endeared himself to the local fan base and went 129–140 in 2004–05.

Sam Perlozzo, who was from nearby Cumberland, Maryland, was promoted from bench coach for the 2005 season. He also lasted two years, going 122–164. Finally, Dave Trembley took over as interim manager on June 18, 2007, when Perlozzo was fired. Trembley had some success and eventually had the interim tag removed. However, he never won enough games to last more than three seasons and he was fired on June 4, 2010, after going 187–283 over his tenure. Juan Samuel took over as another interim manager before Showalter was subsequently hired.

The losing, however, was not the only thing that stung the fans. As the Orioles began to lose, the Yankees continued to win. The Red Sox also enjoyed a renaissance. Each of those storied franchises have fans around the country, and as each team won, those fans flocked to visiting stadiums to support the players. Camden Yards became ground zero for many of these fans. As a result, the Orioles' audience suffered the indignity of having their stadium completely taken over whenever the Yankees and Red Sox came to town. A fan was once pictured in *The Baltimore Sun* carrying a sign that read: "Fenway Park at Camden Yards."

Many Orioles fans blamed Angelos for these problems. They contended that if Camden Yards was full of fans, even if they supported the opposing team, the Orioles organization made money. They worried the franchise no longer even cared about winning. As more Yankees and Red Sox fans helped sell out Camden Yards, more Orioles fans stayed away, rather than be taunted in their own city. Those games against the AL East foes also became more premium on the schedule, which meant they cost more to attend as opposed to a game against the Royals or Mariners.

The attendance problem got even worse when Major League Baseball allowed the Montreal Expos to relocate to nearby Washington, DC, for the 2005 season. This created another huge controversy because the Orioles said a big portion of their fans came from the DC suburbs and helped drive attendance at Camden Yards. As a result, the Orioles said they owned the Washington market and the local presence of a second team would be financially devastating.

Despite Angelos's concerns, the Expos were allowed to relocate. In efforts to help soften the blow of two franchises within fifty miles of one another, MLB allowed the Orioles organization to create a regional television network called the Mid-Atlantic Sports Network, or MASN, that would broadcast both teams. This meant the Orioles would keep the yeoman's share of profits made from television. This was a controversy that would boil for years to come and eventually became a contentious court battle.

Nonetheless, the emergence of a team in Washington meant fewer people from the DC suburbs would be coming to see Major League Baseball in Baltimore. Attendance at Camden Yards slowly trickled as the stadium aged and some of the novelty wore off.

In 2001, the Orioles drew 3.1 million fans and ranked sixth in attendance despite finishing the season at 32–98 and 32½ games out of first place. By 2006, that number had dwindled to 2.2 million and Baltimore was ranked 20th in attendance among all major league clubs.

What does any of this have to do with Showalter? For one, he immediately created a buzz when he arrived in 2010. The team also began to move up in the standings, and proved that winning can solve a lot of an organization's problems.

Baltimore drew 1.7 million fans in 2010, falling to 24th on the list. However, when Showalter led the team to the playoffs in 2012, attendance shot back up to 2.1 million. The Orioles then had 2.4 million the following year, and increased again in 2015 to 2.5 million. As the team played better, the city once again embraced them. This also meant fewer Yankees and Red Sox fans able to take over Camden Yards because the local crowd was buying the tickets.

"We've done a better job of keeping that down," Showalter said. "I noticed last year and the year before."

Under Showalter, the Orioles also instituted more promotions to endear themselves to the local fanbase and accepted more responsibility as a team from Baltimore as opposed to representing an entire region. In 2012, the Orioles brought back the cartoon bird on its home and road caps and batting helmets to celebrate the 20th Anniversary Season of Oriole Park at Camden Yards. The new bird borrows elements from the cartoon bird of the '60s and '70s, which were some of the proudest eras in franchise history.

Following the riots in 2015, the Orioles wore Baltimore on their home jerseys for the first time in franchise history. It was a subtle gesture that went a long way with the local fan base.

Perhaps one of the loudest days at Camden Yards since the turn of the century was when Baltimore beat the Red Sox 6–3 on October 1, 2012. Although they had to wait to see if they clinched a spot in the playoffs that day (the Orioles needed the Rangers to beat the Angels to officially earn a spot in the rotation), the victory over Boston set off a raucous celebration among the 41,257 at Camden Yards, which had not experienced postseason baseball in fifteen years. The Orioles then put the Rangers and Angels game on the scoreboard and many of the players and fans stayed to watch. However, another celebration would have to wait, as Torii Hunter gave the Angels the lead with a two-out, two-RBI double in the ninth that sent most of the Baltimore fans and the Orioles back to the clubhouse. Showalter acknowledged the fans' loyalty by waving to the crowd before disappearing into the clubhouse.

"It would have definitely been cool to celebrate with our fans," Orioles slugger Mark Reynolds told the media after the game. "They've been supporting us all year. To be able to celebrate out there with them and take in the moment, it would have been pretty neat."

However, the Orioles eventually would clinch at least a wild card berth later that night when the Rangers topped the Angels 8–7 in the second game of the doubleheader. At the time, the Orioles had a chance to win the AL East if the Yankees stumbled in their final regular season series against the Red Sox. However, the Bronx Bombers swept Boston and took home the division title. Nonetheless, the Orioles were confident they could make a deep run in the postseason. They were especially excited about playing in front of their fans at Camden Yards.

"One is assuring yourself of getting a chair at the dance," Showalter said. "And then we'd like to figure out a way to play some games at our park in front of our fans. It's in our court."

The Orioles, though, had to go through the Yankees in the opening round. Game 1 was set for Camden Yards and a sellout crowd of 47,841 watched the Yankees take home a 7–2 victory. However, unlike in recent years, the entire stadium was orange; there was no takeover by Yankees fans. The Orioles then took Game 2 with a 2–1 victory before another orange-clad, sellout crowd of 48,187. The excitement was so great that even the owner, Peter Angelos, made a rare appearance in the Orioles clubhouse following the game to congratulate the players and soak in the moment that had officially exorcised those fourteen years of losing. It was a gesture not lost on the players.

"It is great that he was in here," Jones said. "Obviously it meant a lot to him as much as it did us and the fans. He doesn't come in here a lot. He takes care of business up there and we take care of it on the field. Hopefully, the next time I see him he will be holding a trophy."

The Orioles would eventually lose the series three games to two. Nonetheless, the team was back in the psyche of the city, which was now fully behind the club. All was forgiven for those many lean years. Winning cures all ills.

The celebration resumed two years later when the Orioles clinched a playoff spot again in 2013. This time, Baltimore won the AL East and would be the second seed in the playoffs. The city was ready for an all-out onslaught on Camden Yards by the local fans to help with the home-field advantage. In the opening game against the Tigers, Camden Yards turned into a sea of orange as fans wore Orioles gear and waved bright towels. The enthusiasm set the tone for the entire series against the Tigers.

In Game 2 of the series against Detroit, Orioles were trailing 6–4 in the eighth inning before Delmon Young delivered a three-RBI double with one out that proved to be the difference in the game. The crowd roared so loudly the announcers on the television could barely speak above the noise.

Baltimore eventually swept the series before losing to Kansas City for the AL pennant. Still, the Orioles had taken back Baltimore. The entire city was in their corner again. Manny Machado, Adam Jones, and J. J. Hardy were being celebrated like former heroes Brooks Robinson, Boog Powell, and Jim Palmer had been. Orioles gear was once again ubiquitous around the city of Baltimore.

Instead of opposing fans taking over Camden Yards, the Orioles have found a swath of their fans in every opposing stadium. Whether it be Boston, Kansas City, or Los Angeles, it is not hard to spot some orange in the stadiums. The most notable road support comes in Washington when the Orioles play the Nationals. Sometimes, you can even hear them yelling "O" during the National Anthem.

When the Orioles visited Washington for a three-game series beginning July 7, 2014, Orioles fans took over the stadium. Baltimore was so loud that Nationals starter Stephen Strasburg complained about how the visiting fans were louder than the home crowd. "Well, maybe someday it'll be different," he told MASN.

Showalter has consistently lauded the Orioles fans for the loyalty. He said losing a game sometimes doesn't really sting until he drives home and sees all of the disappointed fans wearing orange still hovering around the stadium. Showalter is especially grateful for the support when the team travels to DC, fully knowing the contentious relationship between the organizations.

"You realize how big an area this was for the Orioles before our owner was kind enough to let them have a team here," Showalter said. "I understand that a lot of people that are here are people who used to come over to Baltimore. Now, it's just a little shorter trip for them."

Chapter Fifteen

MANNY

Manny Machado opened a new, exciting chapter for the Baltimore Orioles when he was chosen with the third overall pick in the 2010 First-Year Player Draft. Machado was viewed by some as the top position player in the entire draft. Machado, drafted as a shortstop, was ultimately groomed as the Orioles' long-time solution at third base. This move drew obvious comparisons to the path of Yankees slugger Alex Rodriguez. He certainly had the potential to become the Orioles' first homegrown franchise player since Cal Ripken. As negotiations went back and forth to sign the young phenom, Baltimore fans once again braced for the worst. However, various reports said that president of baseball operations Andy MacPhail and his staff were able to sign Machado to a $5.25 million deal just three minutes before the deadline to sign draft selections expired. The move paid off.

Machado surged through the minors and was called up to the big league club on August 9, 2012. The next day he gave the hometown fans a sample of the big things to come, homering twice against the Royals. He was the youngest Oriole in franchise history to have a multi-homer game. Showalter was especially pleased with the potential he had in his lineup. Again, the moment was not lost on the seasoned manager that Orioles fans were seeing something special. However, he cautioned that people still had to be patient with the young third baseman.

"It's one of those nights that you're really honored and lucky just to watch," Showalter said. "I look at it more from a city of Baltimore standpoint. He'll put it behind him and realize there's another challenge tomorrow."

Machado also soaked in the moment as Baltimore fans chanted "Man-ny, Man-ny" almost the same way they serenaded former Orioles Hall-of-Fame slugger Eddie Murray.

"We haven't won in a long time and this ballclub has been winning without me," Machado told reporters after the multi-homer game. "Hopefully, now that I'm up here, I can contribute to the team and help them start winning. Buck brought me up for a reason and it was to help this team. So I'm going to do anything I can to help this team and try to make a playoff [game]."

Machado continued to excel as a player and he would never look back. At just age nineteen, Machado appeared in 51 games (191 at-bats) in the 2012 season, batting .262 with seven home runs and 26 RBIs. Machado also hit his first career postseason home run in Game 3 of the 2012 AL Division Series against the Yankees. He was flawless defensively. The Orioles had their man, but not without some inevitable growing pains.

Machado continued to thrive entering the 2013 season. On May 27, he secured his 40th multi-hit game since being called up from the minors. This milestone tied him with Ty Cobb as the youngest player in history to record that many multi-hit games before his twenty-first birthday. He continued to pound the ball and he hit .310 with 7 homers, 45 RBIs, and 39 doubles midway through the season, earning a spot on the 2013 American League All-Star team.

His season, however, came to an abrupt end on September 23 when Machado injured his left knee against the Rays. Machado got hurt running to first after hitting a single. His left leg appeared to awkwardly buckle after touching first base. He fell to the ground and was eventually carted off the field. Shortly afterward, Showalter announced the end to Machado's season.

"Manny's pretty down, as you can imagine," Showalter said. "But Manny will play for the Baltimore Orioles again at a very high level, and I'm real proud of him."

The Rays' players and coaches also showed concern and stood atop their dugout steps as Machado was carted off the field. Tampa Bay manager Joe Maddon took time to reflect on the injury after the game in which the Rays won 5–4.

"That's horrible. Baltimore has really ascended over the last couple years, and he's really been a cornerstone of that whole thing," Maddon said. "I hate to see that. He's a young man, tremendous talent. I don't know him that well, but I think he's got a great joy for the game also. So you hate to see that happen."

Machado underwent reconstructive knee surgery two weeks later. He would be out at least four to six weeks. On the bright side, Machado was expected to be ready for Opening Day in 2014. His season ended with him batting .283 with 14 home runs and 71 RBIs. He also led the American League with 51 doubles and 667 at-bats, despite missing the final two weeks of the season.

When spring training arrived prior to the 2014 regular season, the Orioles wanted to take their time with Machado and the knee injury to make sure he was fully healthy. He missed almost the entire first month of the season before being activated on April 29. He showed no lingering effects of the injury and thrived both defensively and offensively.

Just over a month after his return, Machado was also forced to deal with his first big controversy. In a game against

Oakland on June 7, Machado took exception to the way A's third baseman Josh Donaldson tagged him during a force out. The two exchanged words, forcing both benches to empty, but no punches were thrown. Machado did not back down, saying the tag was a bit emphatic. Of course, Showalter defended his player.

"I think sometimes you're off balance and you've been through some of the things he's been through with his knee, I can see how you might be sensitive to that," Showalter said. "And I also see how their guy's trying to make sure he applies the tag, so got two passionate people. Manny cares. And until you've walked a mile in a man's shoes, you really don't know what goes on, but it's a pretty easy call for me what side of the fence I'm going to sit on."

The contention, however, did not die down and carried over to the next game with the introduction of a new incident. Machado, on the backswing, made contact with the head of Oakland catcher Derek Norris in the sixth inning, forcing Norris to leave the game. Two innings later, in apparent retaliation, Oakland reliever Fernando Abad twice threw inside to Machado, prompting Machado to throw his bat down the third base line and the benches emptied again. Both Abad and Machado were ejected from the game in which the A's went on to win 11–1. Machado pleaded innocent.

"The bat slipped out of my hands," he said. "Trying to make contact and the umpire thought it was intentional and he tossed me at that point."

Nonetheless, Machado issued a formal apology the next day. Machado said, "I want to apologize to all my teammates, my coaching staff, the entire Orioles organization, and Oakland and to my fans for the way I acted. That's not the way we play baseball around here." As far as Showalter and the Orioles were concerned, the incident was over and everyone was ready to move on. Major League Baseball had other ideas and suspended Machado five games. Abad avoided a suspension and was simply fined $750 for throwing at Machado. Showalter took issue with the way Machado was ultimately handled.

"He's a 21-year-old young man that made a mistake, and he's done the right thing since then to move forward with it the way it's supposed to be done," Showalter said. "Now there are some more steps involved before we can put it behind us."

After missing the five games, Machado returned to the starting lineup and continued to produce. However, a season full of challenges for the young phenom continued when Machado sprained his right knee on August 11 against the Yankees. In the second inning, Machado hit a broken-bat grounder to shortstop but collapsed in the batter's box. In what initially appeared to be a simple sprain turned into a problem that entailed another season-ending knee surgery on his medial patellofemoral ligament. Both Machado and the Orioles agreed it was best to get the procedure done early so he would be fully ready for 2015.

"I could have waited," Machado said. "It's been 11 days, 12 days now, and not one little sign of it getting better. So, why keep waiting and lose time for next year? Obviously, we're thinking about this year and not next year, but at the same time, it wasn't getting any better. There wasn't anything we could do. The only thing was going in there and fixing it. It's just something that it wasn't getting any better at all."

Machado finished the 2014 season batting .278 with 12 home runs and 32 RBIs over 82 games. Catcher Matt Wieters also underwent season-ending elbow surgery that year. However, Showalter and the Orioles were not about to cave to the adversity.

"It's just reality," Showalter said about the injuries on August 23. "What are you going to do? Say 'Stop, I want to get off'? There's another game today, another game tomorrow.

Third baseman Manny Machado wanted to prove to everyone that he could go the distance, and he did just that in 2015. He played in all 162 games and banged out 35 homers with 86 RBI despite batting leadoff much of the time.

This game has a strange way of finding unexpected heroes, so to speak. It's another opportunity that opens up for somebody, is the way I'd look at it."

The Orioles responded with a magical playoff run without some of their marquee players. Showalter was able to maintain the course. It was an impressive run without the injured Machado and Wieters, and eventually Chris Davis (who was serving a suspension), out of the lineup for the entire postseason.

After missing the back end of the season and the playoffs, Machado was ready for 2015. He had another breakout season and reached a career-high for home runs before the All-Star break. He also participated in the Home Run Derby contest at Great American Ball Park in Cincinnati. He hit 12 homers off Orioles coach Einar Diaz in the first round, but still fell to the Dodgers' Joc Pederson, who went deep 13 times. The next day, Machado hit an RBI double in the seventh inning of the All-Star Game, helping the American League secure a 6–3 victory and home-field advantage in the World Series for the tenth time in thirteen years.

Chapter Sixteen

MARKAKIS AND THEN THE RETURN

Despite the lack of success the Orioles experienced during much of his time with the team, right fielder Nick Markakis always seemed to be a fan favorite, a guy who's not terribly flashy but goes out and does his job every day, and often does it very well. He embodied the blue collar work ethic of the city.

Markakis came to the team in 2006 after being picked in the first round of the 2003 draft. He struggled at first as a rookie, often playing left field in the early days before seeming to settle in when moved to right. He played 26 games in left that season but never went back. Markakis batted .291 with 16 homers and 62 RBIs as a rookie and finished sixth in the Rookie of the Year voting. He quickly became a fixture in the Baltimore lineup, but the Orioles spent most of his first six years fielding teams that just weren't very good.

Still, Markakis became a leader in the clubhouse and wasn't a complainer. He quietly went out there and did whatever the manager of the moment asked. And they certainly asked a lot because the Orioles surely needed a lot in the early days. During the first part of his career, Markakis gave the Orioles plenty of power and hit high in the lineup to help a team that often desperately needed offense to make up for poor pitching.

Markakis really seemed to click with Showalter when the skipper joined the team in 2010. Showalter often talked about how much he liked and respected Markakis—whom he often called "Nicky"—as a person and a player. The Orioles needed a player like Markakis to serve as a clubhouse leader as Show-alter helped change the attitude in the clubhouse and turn things around on the field.

Markakis truly was all about the team with the Orioles. He broke his thumb when hit by a CC Sabathia pitch in September of 2012, and although the Orioles were hopeful the right fielder could return for the playoffs, Markakis didn't make it back in time. Still, he stayed with the team to cheer them on as the young Orioles team found themselves in the playoffs. He later played a big role when the Orioles made it back to the playoffs in 2014.

That ended Markakis's career with the Orioles. In a bit of a surprising move, he signed with the Atlanta Braves when the team offered him a four-year deal in the offsea-son. The Orioles and Markakis had been talking about a new contract, and many were hopeful that the outfielder could remain in Baltimore and possibly finish his career at Camden Yards.

At that point, though, things took a bit of a controversial turn. *The Baltimore Sun* reported that the two sides were close to a four-year, $40 million contract soon after the 2014 season. *The Sun* also said that the Orioles apparently held some worries about an MRI that displayed a bulging disk in his neck. The Braves came in and offered $44 million over the same time period, even knowing that he'd need surgery, and the Orioles didn't appear to want to match that; Markakis took the Atlanta offer.

Losing Markakis hurt the Orioles in a number of ways. The other players on the team certainly did not appear to love the move, which left a big hole in the team's clubhouse.

"You always miss him, the human being as much as the player, and that's saying a lot because he's a good player," Showalter told CSN Baltimore at the end of spring training. "He got a great contract in a great place that really fits for him, and so I'm happy for him and his family. I could say something that would probably get me in trouble, so I probably shouldn't. I'm still thinking he's going to be here . . . no I don't. Will I ever get to that point?"

Showalter often talked when Markakis was with the team about how much he admired the outfielder for who he was and what he did. He mentioned that again in this conversation, and the skipper's sadness at losing him wasn't tough to see.

"I don't want to forget good things that good people, good people [do]. He's a player that played for a team that I managed, but he was more than that. He's a good human being and a good teammate, and we miss him," Showalter said. "That's kind of the coldness of the reality of the way it works. They did something. They wanted him, and they were able to do what they needed to do, what nobody else in baseball, not just the Orioles, could do."

The days leading up to the three-game series in July in which Markakis returned to Baltimore as a Brave—and especially the first game—began to draw some publicity when the normally quiet Markakis admitted that coming back to Oriole Park at Camden Yards while playing for another team would be an unusual, even "weird" type of feeling. He met with media in the Atlanta dugout before the series opening and talked about his feelings. He said the fans could do whatever they wanted in regards to him—boo, cheer, whatever they like. After all, they paid money for their tickets and were coming to watch a game. Overall, Markakis understood the business at hand.

"There are no hard feelings. It's a business and I understand the business side of baseball now," he said in an interview with *The Baltimore Sun.* "I have never been through it before and it's a tough process. And it is tough to process. [But] I'm coming in for three games and I'm going to try my best to win each game and then I'll move on to the next city."

Nevertheless, Markakis said the whole situation was just unusual due to the back story with the Orioles.

"It's different," Markakis said. "I spent nine years here. This is the team that drafted me. This is the team that introduced me to professional baseball. To be gone after so many years, it's definitely different. I am in a good place right now. We have great teammates. It's a great organization. I'm happy where I am right now."

Atlanta manager Fredi Gonzalez put Markakis in the lead-off spot, so he started the game, and an emotional moment began when the right fielder walked towards home plate. Markakis walked from the on-deck circle near the Braves' third-base dugout and crossed paths with Baltimore catcher Matt Wieters, a longtime friend. The two were laughing and smiling for a few moments as the roar from the crowd continued to grow.

The cheering quickly grew into a standing ovation. As a quiet tribute to his former teammate, Orioles starting pitcher Kevin Gausman stepped off the back of the mound, basically saying he wasn't quite ready to pitch yet, so that Markakis could enjoy this moment. As Gausman stood behind the mound, fiddling with a few things, the ovation became even louder, clearly touching the outfielder.

"I mean, that's just one of those things, you've just got to feel out the situation," Gausman said later. "Anybody would have. What he did for this team, for the city. I think it's funny that he was still playing right here. Just kind of weird, kind of different seeing him in a different uniform. But obviously we all love him and respect him. Just one of those guys that did everything the right way. He made it pretty easy."

He stayed outside the batter's box for several moments. The batting gloves went off and on while Markakis kept the bat under his arm. The cheering went on through all of it and kept getting louder and louder. Finally, Markakis looked over to the Orioles in their dugout and then took off this helmet to salute the fans on both sides of the stadium to say a quiet but emotional thanks. He kind of made his thank-you like a salute, and the fans roared again. As Markakis stepped into the box finally to face Gausman, Wieters appeared to be teasing him and both smiled. After that, Markakis, being Markakis, did exactly what he did so many times with the Orioles while leading off the inning. He ran the count full and then slapped a line-drive double to left. Later, Showalter said that he got the ball and was signing it and sending it over to Markakis.

The Orioles went on to a 2–1 victory in 11 innings that night, topping the Braves when Wieters hit a walk-off homer to right-center. After the game, though, one of the first topics of conversation with Gonzalez was the ovation for Markakis and what the skipper thought of it.

"You know what, they don't give people that type of ovation if you're a turd. Let's just put it that way, and you guys clean it up for me if you want to," Gonzalez said. "He's a solid guy. The people here in Baltimore love him. They give that to good people and good players."

Alex Wood was the Atlanta starting pitcher that night, and he also was impressed to see how much the Orioles fans wanted to say thank-you to someone who helped turn things around in Baltimore.

"That's pretty special," Wood said. "People don't realize not every place does that for guys, and for him to have that moment, I'm sure he loved it a lot and appreciated it. For us as players, stuff like that really is awesome."

Wieters expressed similar feelings. He understood the Markakis situation even better than Wood because Wieters played his whole career with the right fielder. That's why watching what happened meant so much to him.

"It was good to see Nick come back and be able to get the ovation from the crowd," Wieters said. "It makes us all feel good in here and motivated to play a good game . . . It is cool, especially the first at-bat. It was cool to see the ovation. I knew Orioles fans were going to give him a great ovation, and I know he appreciated it. Nick does like he always does. He answered it when the time was [right]."

Showalter also was touched by the emotional ovation for his former star. He had joked before the game about how Markakis would probably "get nine hits" in the series (he actually did get five, no surprise there) but really liked how the Orioles fans greeted Markakis.

"It was one of those things where we were all in the dugout wanting to applaud too, but you kind of did it with your heart and not your hands," Showalter said. "Especially when you play [at] so many unfriendly venues, more than just the unfriendly fans, it's nice to get back to this type of baseball environment for our players. It's always a reminder of what we're trying to accomplish and what it means to so many people other than us. We miss him."

Markakis also clearly appreciated the gesture. After the game, he talked to the media about what it meant to him.

"These fans have been great to me my whole career," he told the reporters. "Tonight just shows what type of fans they are. [It] was pretty cool. These people here are great, and it's something I'll never forget."

Adam Jones, the Baltimore center fielder and close friend of Markakis, expressed some frustration that the Orioles were unable to reach a deal with Markakis after he signed with the Braves. "U don't want my opinion!!!!!!!!" is what Jones tweeted right after the deal was done.

However, everyone moved on. In the eighth inning of that first game in the series, Markakis lined a single to right-center that Jones needed to run a long way to gather. The teams were locked in a scoreless tie at that time, and Markakis took an extremely wide turn at first, almost as if he was trying to get Jones to think he might go to second, before turning and going back to first when the center fielder gunned a throw to second.

Jones then had some fun with his old friend. He pointed at Markakis at first and laughed, yelling, "you know better than that." Both players smiled.

Without Markakis in the Baltimore outfield, Showalter and Duquette were banking on the fact that Alejandro De Aza could become an every-day player (or something close to it) in left and newly-acquired Travis Snider might do the same thing in right. De Aza played a big role in helping the Orioles run to the American League East title in 2014 after the Orioles acquired him late.

But he wasn't the same in 2015. De Aza batted just .214 in 30 games in 2015 and never became the player he was the year before, when he hit .293 in 20 regular-season games plus .333 overall in the team's two playoff series. He also struck out an alarming 34 times in 103 at-bats in 2015, and the Orioles ended up trading the outfielder to Boston on June 3.

Snider also didn't come through like the Orioles hoped. He struggled throughout the first four months of the season, especially on offense, never finding the consistency the team needed.

As for Markakis, he did eventually undergo surgery on his neck issue around the time he signed his deal with Atlanta and returned for the start of the season. His offensive production with Atlanta was pretty much the same except for a sharp drop in home runs—he hit just one through the first 100 games—although Markakis had said a lack of offseason work could have accounted for that.

In any case, his tenure with the Orioles is one on which fans could look back fondly.

Chapter Seventeen

TRADE DAY

The 2015 trade deadline again brought some interesting stories to an Orioles team battling for the playoffs. Within their division, the Toronto Blue Jays, made the biggest headlines, completing three blockbuster deals for the stretch run. The Blue Jays acquired ace pitcher David Price from Detroit, All-Star shortstop Troy Tulowitzki from Colorado, and Ben Revere from Philadelphia.

The Orioles usually take a different approach to the trade deadline, tending to stick to a low-key, lower-budget style. They have frequently made "rental" moves, which come when a team acquires someone about to be a free agent but then doesn't sign them for the long term. For example, in 2014, when the Orioles won the American League East, they made a deadline deal for left-hander Andrew Miller. He played a big role in helping the Orioles lock up the division and pitched well in the playoffs. But after the season, he signed with the Yankees and became their closer in 2015, leaving a big hole in the Baltimore bullpen.

Also at the end of the 2014 season, the Orioles had to decide what to do with the three valuable free agents they had

available. Right fielder Nick Markakis, left fielder/designated
hitter Nelson Cruz and relief pitcher Miller saw their contracts end and many fans hoped the team could bring one or
two of them back.

But it did not happen that way. Miller went to the Yankees,
Cruz signed with the Mariners, and Markakis came close to an
agreement with the Orioles but then signed with the Braves.

Naturally, there were back stories behind each deal. While
the Braves offered Markakis a deal the Orioles did not match
after apparently having some concerns about the outfielder's
health, the Yankees signed Miller for four years and $36 mil-
lion, and he reportedly left an even bigger deal (possibly for
$40 million) on the table to go with New York.

Cruz had signed a one-year deal with the Orioles before
2014 for about $8 million. He wanted a longer deal but could
not get one after serving a fifty-game suspension for his role
in the Biogenesis scandal the previous year. Cruz said that
he would have been very happy to stay in Baltimore, but he
wanted a contract longer than the Orioles would offer, and
that's why he signed with Seattle for four years and $57 mil-
lion, according to various reports.

The fact that the Orioles did not sign any of the three
seemed to surprise—and even upset—a bunch of fans. The old
"Orioles are cheap" thing that's been hanging around the team
for a while reared its head, and many fans complained about
it throughout the winter. Since Showalter and later Duquette
came on board, the Orioles haven't made the big-money moves
that teams like the Yankees, Blue Jays, and Red Sox seem to do
in their division. Instead, the Orioles are looking for players
they can pick up—or even "rent" for the final few months—at
a lower cost. That's how they got Miller and other players in
the past few years since becoming a strong team again.

It's also what they did once again in 2015. The Orioles
waited until the morning of July 31—the day of the trade

deadline—before pulling the trigger on a deal that brought them outfielder Gerardo Parra from the Brewers in exchange for minor-league pitching prospect Zach Davies. This was the kind of deal that has become a Duquette signature in recent years. Parra can play left or right field (winning Gold Gloves at both positions) and bat in a number of spots in the lineup. The Orioles began using him near the top of the lineup, filling a hole that they desperately needed to plug. Plus, Parra had been one of baseball's top hitters over the past three months and came to the Orioles riding a fourteen-game hitting streak. He's solid on defense, offense, and has good speed—and the Orioles got him for a minor-league pitching prospect who's far from a sure thing to make the majors. It's the kind of deal that Duquette has pulled off several times during his tenure with the Orioles.

"We're real happy and excited that we were able to pick up Parra," Duquette said. "He's one of the top hitters in the National League this year and he fits the profile of an every-day position player for us. Two-time Gold Glover, he can hit against left- and right-handed pitching, and he's very good at getting on base. He's got some really good numbers at the top of the order, gives us a good set-up hitter and a good defender to play in the field. That should keep our defense strong, help our pitching, and his presence at the top of the lineup should be a real additive. That's an ingredient that we've been missing, and we're glad to have him join us."

The curious move of that deadline day was the trading of right-hander Tommy Hunter to the Cubs in exchange for Junior Lake, an outfielder who the team sent right to Triple-A Norfolk. Some analysts thought the move looked more like a salary dump (Hunter was scheduled to be a free agent at season's end) than anything else. Hunter had transitioned from a starting pitcher—which he was when the Orioles acquired him in 2011 from Texas—to a fairly dependable middle-inning reliever. He also was very popular in the team's clubhouse. He had a wild sense of humor and knew how to make teammates and others laugh. He easily poked fun at himself and did just that right before the trading deadline. Hunter was sitting at his locker a few minutes before the 4:00 p.m. deadline joking about how one part of his locker would be for Cubs stuff (that deal had been rumored throughout the day) and another part would be for other things. Just minutes later, the Orioles came and told Hunter that he was gone.

Showalter talked a little while later about how the Orioles would miss Hunter in the clubhouse and on the field.

"Tommy never had a bad day," Showalter said. "Very infectious personality and he can pitch. He will help the Cubs. It's not that they wanted him more than us. These aren't pieces of meat. You go through the battles that you go through together, the ups and downs, and [it's tough]."

Hunter also wound up being in the wrong place at the wrong time. The Orioles have been trying to develop a number of younger pitchers, but injuries have spoiled aspects of that plan, to those like starters like Dylan Bundy and Hunter Harvey the last two years. But they've found some other minor leaguers who both come cheaper than someone like Hunter and have options. The latter might be the most important for the Orioles because of the system that they've been using the last few years. If a player has options available, they can be sent up and down to the minors without incident. If they don't, then the team that controls their rights must put them on waivers, where another team could simply claim them. This is why the Orioles have used a number of odd strategies in recent years like sending starter Wei-Yin Chen all the way down to Single-A Frederick for just over a week so they could make some moves.

That move with Chen really seemed to upset the left-hander, but he did have options left. Hunter did not and the

trade to the Cubs opened the door for the Orioles to bring
players on to their roster who did have options left. On the day
of the trade, Baltimore called up right-handers Mychal Giv-
ens from Double-A Bowie and Mike Wright from Triple-A
Norfolk. Both pitchers made it into the game that night
against Detroit in relief roles, although Wright injured his left
calf and went on to the disabled list the next day. They then
called up Jorge Rondon from Triple-A Norfolk. He pitched
one day after Wright went on to the DL and then went back
to Norfolk after the Orioles needed to call up starter Tyler
Wilson to start a game in Oakland due to starter Chris Tillman's ankle injury. Hunter could not have been moved at all
due to his lack of options, and the team said they wanted more
flexibility on their roster.

"So now we're going to give [the younger pitchers] an
opportunity," Duquette said. "It's a lot easier to manage your
pitching staff and the workload when you have pitchers on
your staff and in your bullpen that are on option. And then
based on the workload and availability, you can send a player
down to Triple-A and bring up a fresh player. And that's a way
that we've able to successfully handle our pitching staff."

Hunter clearly understood why the team was moving him.
After all, baseball is a business when you get down to the bottom line. He also was saddened at leaving a team he'd been
with for nearly five seasons.

"There's some great times. Just look at the last four years,"
Hunter said. "There's a lot of fun times here, a lot of good
people, a lot of friendships made. Hopefully, they continue
through the years."

The Orioles also needed to make two more moves, one of
which probably didn't surprise many, but still clearly bothered
folks on the team. They designated two players for assignment,
first baseman Chris Parmelee and pitcher Bud Norris. Parmelee had been with the team for only six weeks and got

off to a very hot start at the plate, so hot that he was playing regularly at first base for a while. Showalter felt so confident in his defensive abilities there that the Orioles then moved Chris Davis—who had improved to become a solid first baseman— out to right field to fill in one of the vacant corner outfield spots that had been a problem all season long.

Despite the good start and regular playing time, Parmelee never found his way at the plate. He fell into a long slump and ended up with just a .216 average in 32 games. His defensive abilities never changed, but the Orioles could not keep him in the lineup with those offensive numbers, something that has been a problem for him throughout his major league career.

The Norris decision was probably the one that most did not see coming in the off-season or at the start of 2015. Baltimore acquired him in a midseason deal in 2013 from the struggling Astros. Many around baseball liked Norris's power. He showed a good, live fastball that could move but never could earn a winning record.

In 2014, Norris began the season 3–5 despite not pitching too badly. Then, Norris turned it all around and won four in a row, later won three in a row, and actually lost just once after July 26, finishing the season with a career-best 15–8 record. He also posted a 3.65 ERA, another career-best.

Thus, Showalter chose him to pitch the crucial Game 3 of the ALDS in Detroit. The Orioles stunned the Tigers by winning the first two games of the best-of-five series in Baltimore and were in position to close the door. Showalter had a couple of pitchers ready to start but went to Norris, and the move paid off. He threw 6 1/3 shutout innings, giving up just two hits. That proved to be enough for the win as Nelson Cruz's two-run homer helped the Orioles to a series-clinching 2–1 victory.

Norris had never pitched in the playoffs before, and his words afterward clearly showed his excitement.

"Today was my first day getting out there, different beast. Something I can't wrap my head around right now," Norris said that day. "But it's just something we played since we were kids. You dream of the opportunity to pitch in a postseason game and get to the World Series and so forth. And once again, I was excited to have my number called and go out there and play. I just wanted to go out there and compete for my people and that's exactly what they did for me, too."

Norris started in the ALCS and gave up four runs on nine hits in 4 1/3 innings in Game 2. He came away with a no-decision as the Royals beat the Orioles and took a 2–0 lead in the series.

The Orioles were counting on big things from Norris in 2015, but it just did not happen. Opposing teams pounded him in spring training. Norris and the Orioles both said they weren't worried and that everything would change in the regular season. It didn't. In fact, sometimes things were worse; Norris just didn't seem to have the power or poise that he'd routinely shown in 2014. The Orioles eventually moved him to the bullpen to make room for Kevin Gausman in the starting rotation and eventually designated him for assignment on July 31. The Orioles had Gausman at the ready. Showalter discussed the decision to let go of Norris.

"He was very instrumental in our success last year, and it's a real reminder about how things snowball mentally and emotionally," Showalter said. "He's physically fine. Someone's going to pick him up, and he's going to pitch well for them. I think Bud needs a fresh start, and he's going to pitch well for whoever picks him up and he's going to pitch well for somebody next year. He just never really got going from spring on. He's got some real good pitching ahead of him. It just wasn't going to happen here."

These are the kind of moves that the Orioles have been making at the trade deadline under Showalter and Duquette.

Since they don't spent money as freely as other teams, the Orioles are careful, as noted before, to look for the bargains that fit them at that time. Showalter has managed to make this strategy work, in most cases. He takes the players that Duquette provides and works them into the lineup in some form.

Chapter Eighteen
THE END OF THE ROAD

Showalter was admittedly sad on October 4, 2015.

Even though the Orioles had just completed a three-game sweep of the playoff-bound Yankees, there was disappointment over not making the postseason for a second consecutive year. A tumultuous season had come to end and there was uncertainty about the direction of the franchise.

Left-hander Wei-Yin Chen, catcher Matt Wieters, first baseman Chris Davis, reliever Darren O'Day, right fielder Gerardo Parra, and left fielder Steve Pearce were pending free agents. Because of budget constraints, there was much uncertainty whether the Orioles would be able sign any of these players, especially Davis, who led the league in home runs.

The Orioles had been officially eliminated from the playoffs earlier that week when visiting Houston beat Seattle 3–2. Until that happened, manager Buck Showalter and the players had refused to give up hope in qualifying for a third postseason berth in the past four years.

"The first time you see those boxes in the clubhouse, it's not fun," Showalter said on September 28. "I haven't see those in the last couple of years."

The Orioles had been in the hunt for much of the season. However, a four-game sweep by the Minnesota Twins in mid-August proved devastating to a late playoff push. By late September, Baltimore was just trying to avoid a losing record.

Entering the final two series of the season against the Blue Jays and the Yankees, the Orioles needed to win six straight games to finish over .500. They didn't accomplish that goal, winning five of six to end the year at 81–81.

Showalter had the team playing hard to the final pitch. In the final game of the season, Davis homered twice in a 9–4 victory over the Yankees. Showalter was proud how his team responded.

"They just don't give in," Showalter said after the game. "I was kidding them that they're my cup of coffee every day because regardless of how you come in or out, they come in the next day ready to play. Everybody feeds off that—coaches, teammates. Their competitive fire never wavered. We looked at everything that happened, the self-inflicted challenges, and that's why, because they're such an accountable bunch."

The last day of the season was an appropriate time to wax nostalgic about the past six months. It's a long journey from the gulf winds in Florida during spring training to the first fall chill that creates excitement for baseball's playoff contenders and uncertainty among the teams looking ahead to next season.

As Showalter addressed the media in his final postgame news conference, he acknowledged the uncertainty moving forward. Would the Orioles be able to sign that valuable group of players? Was it time to go back into rebuilding mode? Showalter didn't so much publicly lobby for the front office to get some deals done, but he was not reticent about the value of players, like Davis and Wieters.

"You're trying not to dwell on it [during the game] because you have a job to do," Showalter said. "But anybody who says,

'No, I just pass it off,' nobody's that cold. You spend as much time together as we do and go through, I don't want to say battles and fights. . . . But it's more than just somebody picking your friends for you. It's become quite a family, something that I really wanted to do when I came here—make everybody feel like they had a stake in this."

With each winning season with Showalter at the helm, the fans made their way back to Camden Yards and the stadium was full of excitement. It was not uncommon for Showalter to admit after a loss how he felt mostly bad for the fans, especially when he saw a bunch of orange shirts around downtown Baltimore as he made his way home.

So, a fall without playoff baseball was another disappointing moment for him.

"You just try to play better baseball and remind everybody how great this place is and can be," Showalter said. "Every time there's the first hint of fall in the air, I want people thinking about playoff baseball and the World Series. That's why we get up in the morning, that's why you go to spring training, that's why you do the things we're going to do between now and February."

Even when things looked bleak and the Orioles went through several challenging stretches, the players never quit on Showalter. Everyone played to the final pitch. And when the season ended without a playoff berth, there was no pointing any fingers.

Davis was especially impressive, and the cherry on top seemed to be his two homers in what might have been his last season in the black and orange uniform of the Orioles. The homers were also a harbinger because they could have been particularly appealing to one of his potential suitors in the off-season. The moment was not lost on the slugger, who publicly said he would like to remain with the team.

"Driving in today, I said, 'Man, this might be the last time I'm making this drive,'" Davis said about the trip from his Baltimore home to Camden Yards. "Just times throughout the day, I wasn't trying to dwell on it. When I was walking down the tunnel, that hit me hard. I actually asked Matt [Wieters] before the game started, I said, 'Is it starting to get to you a little bit?' [He said], 'Yeah.' When I was walking down the tunnel, I thought it might be the last time I do this. Hopefully, it's not."

Fans chanted "Re-sign Davis" in the ninth inning. In just four-plus seasons with the Orioles, he was already entrenched in club history, having hit 161 homers as an Oriole, which was 10th on the franchise's all-time list.

Earlier that week, the Orioles watched the Toronto Blue Jays celebrate an AL East Division crown with a 15–2 victory as part of a double header at Camden Yards. It had been almost a year since the Orioles celebrated their own division title.

"Congratulations to them. They earned it," Showalter said. "We had something that people came after and they took it from us."

Despite the indignity of watching Toronto overtake them, the Orioles responded by winning the second game of that twin bill 8–1. The Baltimore players refused to go quietly into the good night.

Days later, Showalter was impressed as his team put together a five-game winning streak to end the season. The skipper was especially impressed with Davis's second homer of the game against the Yankees in the season finale. That served as a tip of the a cap to the loyal fan base who had to "wait 'til next year" to start another World Series run.

"That's a little too apropos, the last one," Showalter told reporters after the game. "As it left the ballpark, I just went, 'Really?'" To put an exclamation point on the quality of contributions he's had. It's been fun to have a great seat to watch him. He's been very good for our city. He's really established himself here in Baltimore. I felt very honored to be part of that. It's never goodbye, it's see you later. That's the way I always approach the end of the year."

In the following days, the focus would continue to be on Davis. The fans were watching closely to see how committed the team was to winning in 2016. The Orioles had already let Nelson Cruz leave as a free agent the previous season. Despite Showalter's leadership and prowess as a manager, he still needs talent to compete. This was a dynamic not lost on the players.

"From the season we had, losing Nelson Cruz and Marka-kis, we've got to do something," Machado told reporters as players cleaned out their lockers for a final time. "I think our top priority will be signing Davis and try to get a couple more key pieces to stay here as well. I think we've just got to get them back to be where we need to be. Losing Davis is defi-nitely not going to help us."

Management knew the importance of re-signing the team's best players. There were also other major holes to fill, complicating matters even further. The Orioles would still need to also bolster their starting pitching, especially with their top arms in the minors enduring injuries and uncer-tainty with the future. On July 2, 2013, the Orioles traded a struggling young pitcher named Jake Arrieta and Pedro Strop to the Chicago Cubs for Scott Feldman and Steve Clevenger as a way to bolster their roster. Arrieta would find his potential with the Cubs and eventually was named the National League Cy Young Award winner in 2015 after going 22–6 with a 1.77 ERA and leading the Cubs to the playoffs.

None of the Orioles' pitchers on the major league ros-ter or minors could match that type of production. Duquette would have to look outside the organization for help. The dirt had barely settled on the infield and Baltimore was already dealing with the challenges of the offseason in a league that had a distinct financial hierarchy.

"If we're going to improve our pitching staff, we're going to have to add to it," Duquette said after the 2015 season. "You'd love to have a top-of-the-rotation starter. We're going to have to develop players we have and look at the trade market."

Showalter would surely have some input on any free agent acquisitions. When asked just 24 hours after the season ended when the Orioles would get back to work, Showalter confidently replied, "We've already started."

Chapter Nineteen

THE SHORT SLUMP THAT CRUSHED A LONG SEASON

The Baltimore Orioles fell apart in the final six weeks of the 2015 season. Dreaming of the postseason once more, the Orioles simply stopped making the right plays at the right times in so many ways, and instead of making the playoffs, they needed a late rush to finish just at 81–81. They made the .500 mark for a fourth straight year but it proved a bitter pill to swallow since the team came so close to the World Series just one year before.

This season began to fall to pieces when the Minnesota Twins came to town on August 20. The only time Minnesota, a surprising team in its own right, would come to Oriole Park all season turned into a disaster for Baltimore. In the opening game, the Twins crushed the Orioles 15–2 before winning three one-run contests to sweep the series. But what happened in the finale symbolized both the series and how the Orioles fell apart in this season.

Starter Kevin Gausman gave up two runs on three hits in the top of the first, and it was almost like an audible groan went through the Sunday afternoon crowd. After that, though, Gausman gave up nothing else. He retired 17 in a row, which gave the Orioles time to rally and take a 3–2 lead in the fifth inning. Gausman allowed nothing else but those two runs and three hits and made it through seven innings in one of his best performances of the season. Eventually, the game went into the hands of the team's bullpen, usually so reliable but having a hard time in this series.

Set-up man Darren O'Day came on in the eighth and easily retired the Twins in order, two days after giving up three runs in the eighth that let Minnesota escape with a 4–3 victory in that game. Closer Zach Britton came on in the ninth and everything fell apart. An infield single, a soft grounder, and then a single to left with two outs let the Twins tie the game and forced extra innings.

The Orioles tried to rally in the bottom of the 11th inning. J.J. Hardy got a one-out single to left, moving slowly thanks to a sore groin that had pained him for days. Hardy gamely tried to play through it for a while but went on the disabled list after this game. In fact, Hardy, trying to rest the injury, didn't even enter this game until the ninth inning as a defensive replacement, but now was being forced to run, which did not help his situation. Showalter then had no choice but to remove Hardy after Gerardo Parra lined a two-out single to left. Hardy could be the winning run but would have to be sprinting, another thing that would not help the injury.

So Showalter put in Jimmy Paredes to pinch-run at second, but the Orioles left him there when Adam Jones struck out to end that threat. That made things even tougher for the Orioles because now Showalter would be forced to put Paredes into the game on defense. Paredes had his best major league season at the plate in 2015, hitting .275 with 10 homers and 42 RBIs in 104 games—all career bests.

Paredes, a late-season pick-up in 2014 who helped the Orioles en route to the American League East title with some key hits, could be an offensive threat at any time. His defense, however, was another story. The Orioles kept him at designated hitter most times, and his glove didn't get much use. In fact, Paredes played just 17 games in the field all season, and when his bat cooled during the second part of the season, he lost his spot in the line-up and spent lots of time on the bench.

Showalter had no choice in this game but to put Paredes in at third base and move All-Star third baseman Manny Machado over to shortstop. This was all about the numbers. Showalter already had used Ryan Flaherty and Hardy at shortstop. There wasn't much else the skipper could do other than put Paredes in, and third base was the somewhat safer move.

Showalter often jokes about the "baseball gods." Well, they must have been mad at the Orioles on this day, and it did not take long to see that. Minnesota shortstop Eduardo Escobar hit a one-out grounder towards Machado at short, and the ball just hopped right past him. Escobar easily made it to second base, the two-base error putting a runner in scoring position with just the one out. Orioles left-hander Brian Matusz retired the next batter before Shane Robinson grounded one towards Paredes at third. He misplayed the ball, which made it into left field. Escobar scored easily on the error to give the Twins a 4–3 lead. And that's how they won the game.

The Orioles clearly were not a happy group after this one. The combination of being swept at home by Minnesota—the Orioles actually lost all seven games versus the Twins in 2015—and the crazy ending simply infuriated Machado. He's usually got a good attitude, even after bad things happen, but the young third baseman was seething with anger when asked about what happened on his play in the 12th inning at shortstop.

"I'm just trying to make a play, and I missed it," he said angrily. "I know you guys want to write about it. I know you guys are going to start writing on all the stats and the velocity of the ball and all that. It's baseball. It's [expletive] baseball. We

Third baseman Manny Machado has a great smile and loves to laugh, but his fiery side certainly came out a few times in 2015.

have to go out there and make [and] catch the [darn] ball and there's nothing to it."

In the end, Machado was right but the players weren't happy after this one. And why should they feel good? Home games had been their strong point all season while winning on the road proved to be a puzzle the Orioles simply could not solve. At this point and after this game, the Orioles were determined to do what they always did—simply move forward.

That's possibly why Jones tried to keep his answers to the questions about how the team felt then kind of simple. The Minnesota series now was over, and the American League champion Kansas City Royals were waiting—on the road, no less. Jones said his team had to forget about the mess that was this day and series and just move on to the next.

"It's not how I feel like I should, it's about the reality of it," Jones said. "It's good that it happened. It shows how much testicular fortitude these 25 men have. Let's go on the road and handle our own destiny. It's in our hands. It's not in no one else's so we just have to execute."

Showalter also talked that day about the way his team would have to bounce back. As a manager, these are the toughest times. They lost four straight games where three could have been wins.

The skipper said that every day is a test and only the strongest survive. That's what he was hoping to see from his group. Showalter certainly did not think the Orioles were done just yet.

"We've had people try to—what's another expression besides 'write us off?'," Showalter said. "They think this means that and that means this. I know what it looks like, but I wouldn't sell us short. I really wouldn't."

The truth was that the Orioles had started a long slide which would basically remove them from playoff contention. Suddenly, everything started to go wrong in just about every way. They went to Kansas City next, the team that swept them in four games the previous year in a stunning American League Championship Series. That series was about two teams who won with different styles. Showalter felt fine waiting for the three-run homer and didn't use the sacrifice bunt or need to squeeze or do things like that very often. The Orioles did not have to because they simply had so much power in 2014.

They were using the same style in this season, as were the Royals, who eventually won the World Series relying heavily on their ability to manufacture runs, but it wasn't working in Baltimore. The Royals took two out of three from the Orioles as the three-run homers were not coming as fast. In fact, the homers just were not coming as fast. Neither were the hits and runs. The Orioles would be in the midst of a long and mystifying slump that basically crushed their season.

The Minnesota series began a slide where the Orioles would lose 11 of 12 and eventually go 3–15 over a two-and-a-half week stretch. That slump left them with a 65–72 record and 13 games out of first place in the American League East on September 7 after a loss against the Yankees. Two months before, the Orioles were in first place.

The problems involved just about everything. Showalter's offense began sputtering all over the place. The Orioles scored 63 runs in 18 games, an average of just 3.5 per game, and those were hard to come by. Baltimore simply stopped hitting with runners in scoring position, something that proved costly.

After Tampa Bay handed the Orioles an 11–2 loss on September 1, someone from the media asked Showalter if he felt a bit jealous watching the other team put that many runs up on the board.

"We'd like to do that," Showalter said. "We are capable of doing that. But just because they are doing it doesn't remind me of what we are capable of. You go through periods like we are in and they'll be the first to tell you it's been extended.

We just haven't been able to string offense together for a long period of time."

The pitching, especially the starters, also struggled. They just couldn't go deep into games on a regular basis, which taxed the bullpen and even the offense since leads were hard to get and then hard to hold. Shoulder tendinitis sidelined right-hander Miguel Gonzalez for much of September, and he did not win a game in the final two months. But after that bad 18-game stretch, the Orioles slowly tried to bounce back. Showalter worked hard to keep the Orioles focused on the fact that they were still within shouting distance of the second American League wild-card spot even if the division title was gone, and his team rebounded to go 16–9 in the final 25 games.

"It's important for the Orioles to win a game every night regardless of what the consequences are," Showalter said after a late-season game. "It's important for us every night to win a game. You try to do everything you can. You don't think about the consequences of a loss."

In fact, the Orioles pulled back to the .500 mark (76–76) after completing a three-game road sweep of the Washington Nationals on September 24. Those three wins left the Orioles 3 1/3 games out of the last wild-card spot with 10 games to go, not the perfect spot but still alive. But all of that stopped very quickly when the Orioles went to Boston to take on the struggling Red Sox and lost all three games in that series without scoring a run. That ended any playoff dreams.

Still, the baseball gods giggled at the Orioles one more time. They came back to Baltimore for a four-game series with the Blue Jays, who were on the verge of taking the American League East title. Toronto won the first game and then rolled to a 15–2 victory on the second night, forcing the Orioles to watch the Jays clinch the title on their field, a bitter pill to swallow for any team.

"No loss is easy to accept; we weren't crisp to say the least," Showalter said. "It's not disappointing [to watch the Jays clinch]. Somebody's going to. I didn't watch it. I had a lot of work to do to get ready for the second game. Congratulations to them. They earned it. We had something that people came after, and they took it from us."

That left the Orioles with a five-game losing streak and stuck at 76–81, but they rebounded again to win the final two games versus the Jays before sweeping the Yankees in a three-game series. Those final five victories gave the Orioles an 81–81 record and ensured they'd gone four straight seasons without a losing record. It also showed how big that one bad stretch proved to be in this season.

The manager tried just about everything. He moved players here, there, and everywhere, and tried younger guys. Some things worked and some things did not. This wound up not being their season. Showalter just couldn't work his magic this time around.

Chapter Twenty

THE FUTURE

In an interview with Bob Costas on the MLB Network, Showalter confirmed that Baltimore will be his last stop as a Major League Baseball manager. Showalter's contract with the Orioles runs through the 2018 season.

"This is my last rodeo," Showalter told Costas in July 2015. "I'm fifty-eight, going to be fifty-nine here. I ain't getting out of this one alive."

Regardless of whether he wins a World Series, Showalter will be remembered as a great leader, winning Manager of the Year in 1994, 2004, and 2014. His ability to turn the Orioles back into a winner has already made him one of the most successful managers in the history of the franchise.

Showalter was able to endear himself to Orioles fans for not only winning, but for his respect for the franchise and its history. Former Orioles manager Earl Weaver is a historic figure in the City of Baltimore. His cantankerous, aggressive style of managing resonated with the local community. Weaver was 1,480–1,060 in seventeen years as manager of the Orioles. He led the Orioles to the World Series four times, winning in 1970. He also won six division titles. A statue of him was unveiled at Camden Yards on June 30, 2012. When Weaver died on January, 19, 2013, Showalter took time to reflect on his legacy in Baltimore.

"I look back at so many things that happened this year, with the statues and with Earl, and it really makes you realize sometimes that you really don't have control over what's going to happen, which is obvious to everybody here," Showalter said. "I'm so glad we honored him again and obviously we are still trying to get our arms around the different ways we can honor Earl's memory. I look at the No. 4 [plaque] in the dugout every day. I kind of look at it and sometimes I rub it when we need an extra out or a big hit."

Showalter has shown the professional versatility where there always will be opportunities for him, whether it be in the front office or broadcast booth. He understands that greatness is often measured in championship banners, which he made clear to his players, especially Jones, who has created his own lasting legacy with the Orioles.

"It's like I told Adam Jones," Showalter told Costas. "I said, 'Adam, you know, you could have one of those out there one day. But you know what the difference is with all those guys? Every one of them was on a championship team.' That's how you get statues in Baltimore."

When he finally decides to ride off into the sunset, Showalter will be certainly be missed by the media. He's always good to fill notebooks with interesting facts, blunt observations, and humorous quips. Topics in a typical Showalter press conference could range from college football to Japanese baseballs to growing tomatoes. It's often a fun, informal pow-wow. Ultimately, though, Showalter has always had that rare competitive fire that can only be found at the highest level of athletics. He wants to win. And there's nothing that he's wanted more as a major league manager than to bring a World Series back to Baltimore.

Chapter Twenty-One
WINTER 2015/16 FANFEST

The weather was very nice for a mid-December morning in Baltimore. Maybe that's why so many people seemed to be walking up and down Pratt Street, near the Inner Harbor on Saturday, December 12, 2015. But a lot of those people had springtime on their minds. They were thinking Orioles and baseball. In fact, many of them were waiting to get into the city's Convention Center for the club's annual FanFest. The lines snaked around the building with many fans awash in orange and black, although the start of the 2016 season remained 3 ½ months away and many doubts about the team's roster were still front and center. But it didn't matter to this group. They wore jerseys, T-shirts, and hats, painted their faces, and showed support for their Birds.

This FanFest followed a season in which everything fell apart for the Orioles late in 2015 and they finished at .500 after having dreams of going to the playoffs. The previous winter's lack of movement on the free-agent front upset many who felt the team should not have lost Andrew Miller, Nelson Cruz, and Nick Markakis. They complained about it throughout 2015, and that anger could be seen regularly on social media and heard often on talk radio. But many of those fans remained just that—fans. They were looking forward to Fan-Fest because it gave some the chance to question Showalter and Duquette about what the team would do in the offseason, and what the 2016 team might look like.

That's a tough job for those two to handle. Fans will ask questions in a very blunt manner and rarely can get an answer they like. Duquette especially needed to be like a good poker player in those situations because the Orioles were still in con-tract talks with a number of players, and what do good poker players do? They rarely show their hands. The Orioles had just made a stunning seven-year, $150 million offer to try and get Chris Davis back. But Davis's agent is Scott Boras, who has long been known for waiting to get his clients signed, as that's a better way to bring in a better deal. In fact, he told *The Bal-timore Sun* several days before that he's not going to draw any lines in the sand when it came to a timeline for the Davis situ-ation. Meanwhile, the Orioles said they really wanted to have a big chunk of their roster locked up by Christmas. That line was officially drawn in the sand.

So after just a few days, while at FanFest, Duquette offi-cially told the media that the offer to Davis wasn't just what one media member termed "long-standing." No, Duquette said, it was officially off the table. And that raised more than a few eyebrows. Were the Orioles kind of playing a game of chicken with Davis? In other words, sign it right now or no more offer. The Orioles rarely made long-terms offers of this magnitude to free agents, even ones they were about to lose. That's why the subject of Davis came up several times at Fan-Fest. Showalter joked that there was a bucket off to the side where fans could chip in with coins and money to keep Davis, if they liked.

Darren O'Day was another subject that came up several times. Various social media reports had come out in the days before the event that the Orioles would bring back their All-Star set-up man thanks to a four-year deal. But O'Day then put out a tweet saying basically "hold on, not there yet." Duquette told the fans that day and then the media that they were almost there but not quite done yet. There was a lot of speculation on why but Duquette would not give the reason. Still, the GM's tone when talking to the fans made it clear that the Orioles did not seem too worried. And they were right on the money because they announced the deal a few days later.

O'Day quickly become a fan favorite in Baltimore and said he still kind of shakes his head at the chance he's received— especially with the Orioles.

"I didn't think I'd get a chance to play professionally, [having] been designated [for assignment and] changed teams four times without being traded," O'Day said in an MLB.com article on December 15 when the team announced his signing a few days after FanFest. "It's been an interesting ride, it really has. Baseball's about being ready for opportunities and taking advantage of them when they're presented. I've been lucky enough to do that. I've been lucky enough to have some great help along the way."

However, one of the interesting parts of FanFest was when the fun came out. Fans and children were able to talk straight up with the Orioles and ask questions that would give everyone a peek into their personalities. Fans watch the games all the times but don't really know who people like Showalter are—what makes them tick. Where do they like to eat? What do they like to read? Children are not afraid to ask those kids of questions.

One child asked Showalter a question that had absolutely nothing to do with baseball but still managed to make many in the room laugh, as reported in a video from MLB.com. The little boy went up to the microphone, thought about it, and said: "would you rather have the power to turn invisible or fly?"

The question clearly flummoxed the skipper for a few moments. He thought about it, picked up a bottle of water, and took a sip before giving a short answer that caught the room's attention.

"Both," he said.

Another question came from a child who wanted to know what the manager's favorite holiday was each year. This also was a query that puzzled the skipper a bit. He ran through a bunch of holidays before settling on Mother's Day.

"That's pretty cool," he said in another video.

Still, it was another question from a little girl that really caught the attention of a few of the Orioles and later on, the manager. This girl strode right up to the microphone and asked why Showalter doesn't smile more. Now, she asked this question of starters Miguel Gonzalez and Chris Tillman. Gonzalez, who is a very low-key personality himself, simply burst out laughing. Tillman, the big right-hander, started smiling right away before taking on the question.

"He's always smiling," Tillman said in a video. "He's always thinking. He puts on a front." Tillman also suggested asking that to Showalter.

The answer was a good one, but this young lady wanted more. So she came back later and asked Showalter the same thing. That one also seemed to catch the manager a bit off guard, so he tried to think about it for a moment. He tried to explain to the little girl that because the job he's doing requires a lot of concentration, people might not see him smile as much. But he certainly does plenty of it during games.

"I laugh a lot," he eventually said, as reported in another video. "It's a very serious time. I belly laugh once or twice a game. Adam Jones cracks me up. I have my moments. I'm very serious about what we're trying to [accomplish] there. I smile a lot—trust me."

Those questions give a good look at what FanFest is all about. These are fans who love the Orioles and are especially interested in Showalter and players like Adam Jones because those are the ones they see all the time when watching the Orioles on TV or if they go to the ballpark. This is the kind of event that gives the fans a brief chance to connect with those they watch all the time yet don't even know—and the fans clearly have a blast doing it.

But the event clearly has two focuses for the fans. This year, since it was moved up a bit earlier, before the team made all of its off-season moves, that subject came up in several ways. That's probably not something that Showalter, Duquette, and others enjoyed talking about several times but they handled it well. Still, the management and players understand the importance of the fans in this situation. The fans have really come back since Showalter took over the team and made it better again. There's more of an interest than before when the team

Orioles manager Buck Showalter watches during an afternoon game. He's slowly become the face of the franchise.

was losing all the time, and fans from New York and Boston regularly filled the park.

So it may have been winter, a long way away from the first pitch of the first game, but the truth is there was a lot of laughter that day. The Orioles were good with the fans and answered questions in a smart manner. Still, Showalter was the man that most wanted to see and talk to and talk about. He's slowly become the face of the franchise, no matter what time of the year it is. That's why he was so busy at this event once more.

It's also why, even though you could see so many fans wear jerseys to honor Adam Jones or Chris Davis, others had on Showalter tops. He's known and respected and quite popular already in Baltimore. Wherever the skipper was at FanFest, the fans showed up. That's something that will not change during his time in Baltimore.

Chapter Twenty-two
LOOKING AHEAD

Editor's Note: When this chapter was written, the 2015 calendar year had just come to a close, and Spring Training 2016 games remained a few months away. This chapter includes coverage of trades and transactions that occurred up to the end of 2015 and into the first month of 2016.

There was no controversy at the end of the 2015 season like the previous year. Orioles executive vice president, baseball operations Dan Duquette was not being wooed by another organization like he was by the Blue Jays in 2014. Toronto had moved on by hiring a new president and CEO in Mark Shapiro, which meant that Duquette would not be heading north of the border to a team in the same division. It helped that the Orioles did not have an uncertainty like that one hanging over the offseason this time around. Many fans were still upset that Duquette didn't immediately quash Toronto's interest in him the prior season and some thought the distraction hindered the club's ability to sign quality free agents last winter, especially since the team let Nick Markakis, Nelson Cruz, and Andrew Miller walk away to other teams via free agency.

This time around, Duquette was fully committed to helping the Orioles improve. The 81–81 season of 2015 stung on
many fronts, and the Orioles did not want to repeat that in
2016. Showalter simply waited in the wings as deals unfolded
to see what players he'd have on his roster. The skipper was
prepared to move ahead with the players who showed up for
spring training. Showalter publicly said in the offseason he
doesn't want to be part of any player's financial negotiations.
However, Showalter did say the team needed to improve the
starting pitching. The Orioles had power and defense but
their starting pitching proved inconsistent in 2015 and arguably was what hurt their bid for a second straight division title
the most. The starters just could not go long enough or be
effective enough.

The Orioles organization, as a whole, planned to be busy
with improving the team but faced major questions right
from the start. What would happen with catcher Matt Wieters,
for example? Duquette struck early by acquiring first baseman Mark Trumbo and left-hander C. J. Riefenhauser from
the Seattle Mariners in exchange for catcher Steve Clevenger. Trumbo was the centerpiece of the deal. He averaged
18 homers and 64 RBIs over six MLB seasons. The right-
handed Trumbo was expected to be even more effective in the
hitter-friendly confines of Camden Yards.

"The addition of a proven major league hitter like Mark
Trumbo today lengthens our lineup, and it gives us another
hitter in the lineup who can hit both left-handed and right-
handed pitching and in Mark's case, he can hit the ball out of
our ballpark," Duquette said.

That early splash can set the tone for the offseason. The
Orioles were showing the fans they were committed to
improving the club. Baltimore also made another positive move
by re-signing reliever Darren O'Day to a four-year, $31-
million deal, reportedly beating out the Washington Nationals

to do so. O'Day established himself as one of the premier set-up pitchers in all of baseball and made the All-Star Game in 2015. O'Day might have been able to land a job as a closer at another organization and had several offers on the table. However, he valued his time in Baltimore and how the organization helped him become a better pitcher. O'Day also liked the way Showalter led the team during his time in Baltimore.

"Buck's not going to blow anybody's arm out," he said. "So a short start can affect a team for quite a few days if you don't have the proper safety net in the bullpen."

The signing of O'Day was also huge for Showalter to effectively manage the bullpen. O'Day offered insurance as a closer if there were any injuries to left-handed closer Zach Britton. Showalter was especially impressed with the signing of O'Day, saying the pitcher wanted to return the commitment the team made to him.

"He wants to be a really good pitcher for the Orioles for the next four years and maybe beyond that. He'd like to finish here," Showalter said.

Over his career, O'Day appeared in 273 games for the Orioles, which is the most among the team's active pitchers. The franchise's all-time leader is Jim Palmer, who appeared in 558 games. Catching Palmer is another goal for O'Day, even though the Hall of Fame starter was a right-hander and pitched with the Orioles for about two decades.

"If I have some success over the life of this contract, I might be able to sneak up on Palmer's for the most games pitched in, which, for a starter, is crazy," O'Day said. "To be able to creep up on the leaderboard of such an historic franchise would be very special to me."

In addition to O'Day, the Orioles also re-signed catcher Matt Wieters, who was long-considered one of the pillars of the franchise. Wieters was drafted by the Orioles with the fifth overall pick in the 2007 MLB draft. He had a meteoric rise to

Manager Buck Showalter and catcher Matt Wieters have a good relationship. Wieters is like another manager on the field. It's why he's so valuable to the Orioles—and Showalter.

the majors and became the every-day catcher in less than two years. Wieters is one 24 players in Orioles history to hit 100 home runs. He is also a three-time All-Star, and has won two Gold Glove Awards. Since 2009, he has caught 130 runners trying to steal a base—the best mark in the American League.

Wieters, twenty-nine, accepted the Orioles' one-year qualifying offer for $15.8 million, a move that surprised some as his agent, Scott Boras, hadn't had a client take a qualifying offer previously. But in some ways, what happened to the catcher in the last two years kind of pushed him to that decision. Wieters played just 75 games over the 2015 season after undergoing Tommy John Surgery during 2014. The Orioles held out some hope that he'd be back for Opening Day but he never was able to take back the everyday job despite playing well. He batted .267 with eight home runs and 25 RBIs over 258 at-bats.

As for the Orioles, they loved having their field general back again. How could they not? The Orioles valued Wieters's rapport with the pitching staff, his bat in the middle of the lineup, and his leadership in the clubhouse. Over his seven years through 2015 with the Orioles, Wieters batted .258 with 100 home runs and 371 RBIs

The Orioles did not stop there and even looked overseas to find more talent. The team picked up South Korean outfielder Hyun-soo Kim with a two-year, $7 million deal. Over nine seasons with the Doosan Bears, Kim hit .318 with 142 homers and 771 RBIs. Duquette saw a tremendous upside with Kim as a starter or platoon at one of the corner outfield spots and was confident Showalter would find the best way to use him. Kim also gave the Orioles a potentially solid, left-handed bat in the lineup.

That's probably why the Orioles created even more competition for spring training by trading for L. J. Hoes. The versatile outfielder was the Orioles' third-round draft pick in 2008. He was eventually dealt to Houston for right-hander Bud Norris in a July 2013 deal that was a steal at the time. Norris played a big role in helping the Orioles win the 2014 division title and won a big victory over Detroit in the ALDS. Hoes went over to the growing Astros team as a backup. But now, the Orioles reacquired Hoes, a native of nearby Prince George's County, for cash, which was another low-risk, high-reward deal. He can play anywhere in the outfield and his speed is an asset at the bottom of the lineup or as a pinch-runner later in a game. It gave Showalter another player who could get on base.

Finally, in January 2016, the Orioles and Chris Davis were able to come to terms when they agreed to a seven-year contract. It was a move that should help the team for a long period of time, and, of course, it delighted local fans. After some questions, the Orioles finally sent the message fans wanted to get. Duquette made it clear how happy he was when the team announced they'd re-signed their first baseman (to a reported $161 million deal).

Buck Showalter talks with former Oriole Steve Stone, the 1980 Cy Young Award winner, and current team TV broadcaster Gary Thorne.

"It's a historic agreement; it's the most lucrative contract in the history of the club," Duquette said at the press conference. "He's poised and positioned to have a solid career here. I don't know how many places I went this winter where people said 'you've got to sign Chris Davis, you've got to sign Chris Davis.' When you invest in a contract like this, you're investing in people. We're just so happy to have him returning to do his job for the Orioles for many, many years."

Davis has grown into a real force for the Orioles at the plate and he's become a solid defensive first baseman. This year, the power he gives the Orioles will be a huge help in the middle of their lineup. Last season, he rebounded from a slow start to lead the majors with 47 homers and helped carry the Orioles at times when they struggled in the second half. He got hotter as the season went on, and that power proved to be a big part of the team's offense as it was very inconsistent at the plate in the final two months.

Davis said he was very happy to be back in Baltimore. He came to the team from Texas in a trade during the 2011 season and became productive in the lineup right away. Davis has hit 161 homers with 425 RBI in 617 games with the Orioles and became very popular among fans and teammates.

That popularity and success made it tough for Davis as time moved on last season. He repeatedly was asked about whether he would re-sign with the Orioles, a question he really couldn't answer until the off-season. The questions on this issue began coming up almost every day as the Orioles were all but out of contention in the final weeks of the season. Davis admitted it was something he certainly was thinking about.

"As a player any time you get to a place where you feel really comfortable and a place you really feel like it's home, it's always hard when you know that might be coming to an end," Davis said. "At the end of last season, I was going through so many different emotions. We are ecstatic to be back here for a number of years and hopefully kind of continue the tradition of winning that started really from the time I was traded over here."

Davis said he knows there are going to be plenty of expectations set for him now. That's the negative side about signing a big free-agent contract. Fans want lots of production, often thinking that if you get paid that kind of money, huge things should come from it. Some players don't love that thought process, but Davis said that's fine with him.

"I hope there are expectations," he said. "I'm happy to be here for the next seven years. I think that these next few years are going to be a lot of fun, and hopefully very successful years."

Davis said one of the things that should help the Orioles is that this team kind of goes through the season with a chip on their shoulder. And he thinks that could be a good thing.

"We've never been the sexy team, so to speak, the easy pick to win the AL East," Davis said. "I think we kind of like that role. A lot of us are guys that were traded or kind of passed over with by a previous team. For whatever reason [this attitude] works for us."

Showalter did not say much during the Davis press conference, at one point saying that he was excited about the deal finally being done and that the team had a lot of work ahead of them. But at the very end, when all the questions had been answered, Davis took a deep breath, leaned back, and gave the skipper a big pat on the back. Davis clearly was happy to be back with the skipper and the team.

Nevertheless, the question heading into 2016 is what the Orioles will look like overall. At the end of January, the team still needed to fill a spot in the starting rotation—due to the loss of Wei-Yun Chen to the Marlins weeks prior. Gerardo Parra also decided to sign a 3-year deal with the Rockies, so the Orioles were still in need of another corner outfielder. Still, the signing of Davis went a long way with buying the fans' patience. The team is clearly stronger on offense especially due to the return of Davis and Wieters, in addition to the acquisition of Mark Trumbo. This lineup will be tough to pitch through in the middle.

All of those moves were just incremental stepping stones to getting better and trying to reach the playoffs once again. They also showed the Orioles' fan base that the team was not going to stay put in the offseason. The question was how much it could settle down the fans, who still were grumbling about what did not happen the season before. There would still be bigger deals to be made, but this was a good start by all accounts. The team still did not have the financial wherewithal of the Red Sox and Yankees, but Baltimore was finding other ways to get better—a trademark since Showalter joined the team.

Most importantly, the Orioles were getting closer to the goal of establishing a winning culture year in and year out like the teams in the 1970s and 1980s. It all harkened back to the "Oriole Way," whereby the club set a model of excellence for other teams to follow. This not only wins games and puts fans in the seats, but it also becomes an attractive destination for free agents, who are sometimes willing to bend a bit financially for the opportunity to play in a World Series.

When watching the team's Double-A Bowie Baysox team won the Eastern League championship in September, Duquette said that winning begets winning, especially at the minor-league level. During the great success of the "Oriole Way" in the '60s and '70s, they often had minor-league teams that were great winners. Players would make the majors after winning while coming through the system. They'd like something like this once more.

"The good news about the Baltimore Orioles is that the Orioles have a winning culture, and that winning culture in the locker room, under Buck's leadership, is well known by the players on the ball club," Duquette said. "Players want to be in a winning culture where you are supported by the organization, your teammates, you're mentored by the manager and the coaching staff. That's a desirable place to work as a ballplayer."

Appendix A:

Showalter's Tenure Managing the Orioles

Year	Age	W	L	W-L%	Notes
2010	54	34	23	.596	Took over as the team's manager on August 3, 2010.
2011	55	69	93	.426	
2012	56	93	69	.574	
2013	57	85	77	.525	Orioles beat Rangers in Wild Card game, lost to Yankees in ALDS.
2014	58	96	66	.593	Orioles won American League East, later beat Tigers in ALDS, and lost to Royals in ALCS. Showalter was voted Manager of the Year for the second time in his managerial career, the first with the Orioles.
2015	59	81	81	.500	
6 years		458	409	.528	

Source: Baseballreference.com